MAJESTIC MYSTICISM A CELTIC TRADITION

Chronicle XV11

Panagiota Makaronis

KREA PREA Est.2012

ISBN: 978-1-7635366-6-1

Cover design by: Vista Create
Editor; KREA PREA Est.2012
Written in Australia Melbourne Victoria Craigieburn

I dedicate this book to 777
To those who entertained me during the writing of this Scripture!
I smell Gas!
Who Lit it?
You have banged on my walls to get my attention!
Played the victim, Assuming I will fall for that too! The melody to my ears saved me.
Screamed scammed slammed doors even escaped for 7 days.
Assuming you hiding will change the system because I caught you.

You probably thought you will not be caught out! In fact; SEEYA!!!

You dug holes in places that served me well, you even graffitied a red mark in my foot path to let me know your Targeting me!

Thank you, ever so kindly for putting me through hell!

The inspiration is well spread and well served! Lesson Lived Lesson Learnt!

I could not have written Chronicle 17 without you. Obviously, what is meant to be is meant to be. You came & served your purpose to me & Humanity with your conspiracy ways!

Remain a victim to that Agent who hired you! Watch him return & work against you!
Departing ways now!
May your Demons feed you Hell now!!!!
HELLELUIA

Time to STOP! & LEAVE ME ALONE! Your sick & twisted mind, with your sick & twisted head to get ahead; is now dead.

Where you have a sick & twisted obsession with me! It will no longer trap nor trouble you!

I buried the Hatchet,where I planted it in that hole; you dug. Assuming, targeting me will hand you;

A Diamond in the Rough.

PANAGIOTA MAKARONIS

CONTENTS

Title Page
Copyright
Dedication
Epigraph
INTRODUCTION 1
CHAPTER 1 5
CHAPTER 2 15
CHAPTER 3 28
CHAPTER 4 41
CHAPTER 5 53
CHAPTER 6 66
CHAPTER 7 79
CHAPTER 8 92
CHAPTER 9 105
CHAPTER 10 117
About The Author 135
Books By This Author 141

INTRODUCTION

The Majestic Mysticism a Celtic Tradition Chronicle XV11, is the continuation of my Biblical Odyssey Series. How I survived my daily bread. A journal added by my imagination, and the extension to validate my perception. Where my mission took over my vision and created an opposition.

Whether it is a theory or an indication that I have a vivid imagination. The world is what it is and I describing the way I see it will help me remember when where and I how I got there. State the facts, create a peace then pause and reflect. All so I can get back on track and resurrect from a tongue wag.

Some might assume, this is my Conspiracy Theory. Personally, I see it as an analytical critical Analysis. Based on my dogmatic views, how I see society Wholistically. An offering with my mind's eye, added with the third eye. A systematic control towards a trial to review the corrupts birds eye view.

Without a word of lie, if I did not tread carefully; it would have gone out of control. I was anchored cornered without my knowledge. The shock to my system, had me rigid. My mind racing wild. The thoughts that took over had me living in denial.

Wearing a band aid on an open wound.

A stab in the back, left a huge stigma behind. A warning sign, had come to my attention I could sense I was being watched; stalked in my domain trying to push me out of my comfort zone. All I had to was enter that back door and witness cockroaches a stinge in the air.

Letting me know there were magots everywhere ready to blow fly. For the corrupt planted a seed, repeating a new debt; assuming I was a threat. I on the other end, entertaining them with the notion they were winning. In fact, I was digging them in a deeper hole.

Although they were digging for information. An opening for me to plant a seed of my own. An opportunity to hand them a taste of their own scrutiny had come to fruition. A sinister plan that backfired where every momentum will harm those who knew. Having them surrender, handing me; Happy ever after.

I was returning to pursue a key that was stolen from me. I guess the corrupt knew and wanted to harm me before I caught them in the act. It was part of yearning that was summoning me for a return. It was creating a challenge to hand me concept to fail the corrupt completely.

The Perception had changed, it led them to a destination, no power for resurrection. No method in this world, that will Govern it. Even the one that served them in the long run. For the next Generation will not stand for it. For no favours were done here, it was all in the past.

The corrupt were attempting to cast another spell just to get in and redeem another scheme. The present was a no where near it was meant to be. Because the corrupt went way to far stabbing me in the back. Yielding for a challenge to state a fact, space me out.

Handing me the momentum I need, to hit the corrupt with a final redemption. Pausing for a reflection, to see where I went wrong. Repeat repair, it was the only way for me to remain strong. I had to debate what challenge will save me in the end of that trend.

For what it was worth I was handed a key. It left me restoring my energy, feeding off the concept. About to reap a reward. A key that will hand me the remorse, to hold the corrupt hostage. A chaotic event handing me the power to hit the corrupt with force.

It will fail there method completely. For that terrible event, was benevolent, it had me return upstage and contaminate there journey, up to date. Leading them on so I can continue to remain strong; just to hit the corrupt with sage.

This book is not only a constant reminder of my pitfalls but it is part of my daily routine. Where social environment consists of constant interruption from corruption. Just so their conspiracy can continue on. Where my pathway will remain strong and I will keep moving on.

For each day is a blessing to me, and each day offers a new meaning. A new inspiration to serve me a purpose and to serve one to mankind alone. Hand me the chaos I need to read between the lines. I need inspiration there are no limits in confirmation.

While I continue cross my path carrying the crucifixion to life's tribulations on my back;

What can I say, until we meet again!

AMEN

CHAPTER 1

◆ ◆ ◆

TROUBLE IS ABOUT TO HIT THE CORRUPT THREE-FOLD

The energy I was handed had me branded. Silent but deadly, trapped in the middle of a medley. Where the only troubles I had to face, had me causing effects. Replaced with a final sitting, an admiration to restore my energy and feed off the encryption. Waiting for the challenge to restore.

Meanwhile, my energy had me feeding off the adolescence. It gave me the trace and the trial to sacrifice what I thought was part of a dream that had me sitting in denial. A concept that left me separating the key repeating a trace hitting the corrupt with one more chance to repeat and replace.

It had one foot in the door and the other scheming to return for a yearning. A challenge that had me aching for one final thing, a trace that forced me to repeat a challenge that was way past its used by date. Handing me one more key, for I needed to restore my energy for the dream was innocent.

I returned, fixing what I thought needed to be preserved. It had me haunted by the past. Living in the present and making mountains out of mole hills. Assuming the journey was mine, where my prediction was ripened by the divine, an evolution to change the corrupts constitution.

I had no time than the present to return and create a journey of love and hate. Because I became vigorous, and way to brave for the corrupts liking. They saw me as an easy target, a victim to their bravery. They could not wait to return, and hit me with a forthcoming; an event that haunted me.

Leaving me forced to cause and effect, return for one more key; was heaving at me at every final degree. I needed to reclaim, then repeat to a new game just to follow up on a journey that will give me the power to divide and conquer. Then return to hit the corrupt with one more turn of events.

The tables turned and I got to repeat and reap a reward; coming first and last at last. Where it had me gambling what I thought was a dream. In fact, I was chasing a nightmare in-between. The corrupt had planted an upcoming seed. A vision that failed me and had me feed, off the upcoming event.

An impossible task for me to trace, attract a positive

outcome was out of place. Because the journey had me on a pathway of being tongued. I was urged to hit back and finalise the impact. So, when I hit the end, they can hit run leaving me wondering what I did to deserve such a serve in the long run.

I was stuck questioning What did I do to deserve such a hiding! I was missing out on the real picture troubling my mind and waiting for the chaos to subside. For the conclusion had me questioning the corrupts motive. It forced me to retrace, follow up on a case and repeat that faith.

It had me less, likely to accommodate their needs. More likely for I, to gather mine; an attempt, to make my dream a reality. What I thought was part of a trend, was a throwback, to push me off track. An attempt to fail me again, trapped in-between a gap.

A wasted decision, that only existed in the corrupts peripheral vision. It was a pointless act of kindness that had presented me with a final. Where I get in and feed of those who hit me with feedback. Forced to condition the mission and compel another competition.

Restoring my energy in the end, created an edge; A need to have the corrupt return, and pledge finalising that thread. A string of events, that had me warned, based on a condition I could not replace. Because I had to undo and disclaim another force; to change the cause of action.

Requesting a recount was farfetched, for I was given the

short end. A dead end with no luck nor a happy ending to spare me a chance to return. I forced without my blessing to recreate a force to hand me a new cause. There was no recollection t that debt just a hint of a hit that lined me up.

Where the end of that collection was inevitable. It was not going to give the corrupt a chance to recreate a final journey. because the dream took over and I fell into a web lies. Just to get back on track and feed off those who fed off me, returning for one more key.

A challenge that served me well then, cleaned me out now. Those who caused the effects, were nowhere near they were meant to be. Because the journey created a catastrophe. It was a challenge restarted from a past dream. Where I had to return and redeem another scheme.

Just to recreate, a trace to challenge that service that had me cornered. It was unlimited and the access to release that feast had no measure to change that proposal. It had me living in denial, for there was no recollection just a confirmation I hit the end of that restoration.

A report that was poisoning my spirit. It was handing me the resolution, to revolutionise the corrupts position. Without handing them a chance to compete because the competition was based on a past recission. It had no meaning nor did I have a chance to reclaim nor repeat that proposal.

It served me well hit me with a forthcoming spell.

A debt that took me on a journey and created a forthcoming event. It served its purpose back then, turned against me unwillingly now. It put me through hell. A turn of events that messed up my head; restoring the corrupts method again.

I was hunted down, restoring my energy. For those who knew wanted a piece of the action. Hitting me with abreaction it was causing an effect tricking me whenever the corrupt saw a defect. They were on the move, trapping me whenever they saw me easy. Relisted a cover up, resisting me.

Thanking their lucky stars the test was a pointless affair. There was no dream nor drama just a troubled trip down memory lane. It had me afraid to return and hit the corrupt with the same game. For the competition, was part of a wish, with admiration; to hand me deportation.

For the corrupt were desperate for information. Forcing their way in and hitting me with confirmation. A curse to be reversed was upcoming. For they took their time trying to hit me with the same game. It was gambling the wish that served me, an incoming key.

A curse I had to reverse come first, releasing tension; an ongoing condition. It was leaving me, shocked to the system. Forcing my way through, it had me on the edge. Restoring the energy, of those who like to poke around and pledge. While I am sitting on the edge, waiting to be called up.

A turn of events had me on the edge, for I hanging in there, was raiding their heads. For a string of events was stirring the pot. Handing me a chance to restore my energy in advance. Where I got a chance to take advantage of the corrupts final waking moment a challenge that was entertaining.

Walking into the unknown hit me with denial. It forced me repeat and serve the corrupt with a final trial. Just make the sure the corrupt lose the plot independently. It was restoring the key they stole handing it back to me freely. Seen as they hit me at first, I had to reverse condition the mission.

Returning the favour, handed them a final momentum. It stung like a bee, the shock the system hung and strung me along. It left me questioning the corrupts method, because that ongoing cause was part of a cue. An entrance to the unknown, where those who knew needed me to get a clue.

Because I knew they needed me to get through, it served me well. It gave me a chance to reclaim my innocence and gloat; finally steering the boat. By feeding of a test that hit me with a quest, it had me return and reveal another trial where the wheel of fortune come to fruition,

I assumed I was fortunate enough, to see my future unfold. It was handing me a story untold, A challenge that had me read between the lines. It was hitting me in the end, warning me I no longer wish to return nor pretend. Because the case was too harsh to embrace and too easy to let go.

I went far and beyond, to make the outcome stand out. No failure, nor follow up will lead me to a wrong decision. It had me repeating a competition. Referring back to an old curse, a feast I could release and a challenge that held me up and forced me to reveal another stand up.

All I had to was walk my way through a maze, trapped no longer. Nor relive those days living in a daze. For I had footage from above and I knew how to get through. Where every challenge had a reservation and every thought wave was reoccurring with the end about to portray another bad day

When I reached my peak, I could reestablish a new meek. Then concentrate on a journey that will bring peace to my inhumane society. I will continue where I left off, hunting those who knew down. Returning for a favour while I push the corrupt towards a pathway of a vendetta.

My foundation had become solid; and the corrupt were getting itchy. While I was handed the all clear, I was facing another let down. Hitting me with a yearning, had become a warning. It was a scheme, that backfired. Where the journey fell into a dream, that turned into a nightmare.

It was a trace, where the case, was based on a past chase. It was hitting the corrupt in-between the drama. Where the dream was a theme that ended abruptly. Handing me the opportunity to launch for another key. It was the only way I could restore my energy. Meanwhile the unjust created peace.

I was haunted with a feast, forced to release, finalising a piece. While given the all clear, it was part of a trace, that had me meddling someone else's swing of affairs. Where the pendulum had moved side to side, with a rapid circular motion. Warning me, I hit the end of that force; moving forward.

I was competing, with those who remained silent. Sorting it out bit by bit, reclaiming my trace, then relying on one case. Recapping what I assumed was part of a way out. It was giving me the challenges I needed to restore my energy to succeed. All by reinstating my faith in humanity.

I was taken for a fool, led to believe the journey was mine. Where the end was clear and the trace was nowhere near it was meant to be. Because I hit the corrupt with a catastrophe. The trip was to be given to me with a positive intention; Outlining what I thought was part of a trust.

In fact, it was part of a dead end, that handed me a death threat. Hitting back with redemption, was the end. It was a pointless affair, that was taken away with a final; a truth and dare. It had me forced to create a case that caused an effect. It failed the corrupt and hit them with a defect.

It had me erasing the end of that treason, facing another competition. Even though, I knew who they were the end. The result had me on the edge, facing another quest. Preventing the corrupt from returning and hitting me once again. For the challenge they handed me; was part of a trend.

The intention was purely, to fail me in the end. Assuming they had all the answers, and the know how because they assumed their method was more powerful than mine. But the journey they chose was part of the norm. It was creating a test, that forced me to rebel; against the corrupts conquest.

It had me challenging the journey, all while restoring my energy. I was stuck feeding off the conspiracy. While preparing myself for another dead-end. It was leading me towards a journey of feeding off the energy that would have given me the entrance to a virtual reality.

A first and last draw, had become visible once more. Before I hit that encore, I was given a chance to delve into a trance. Then follow up on a key, where I get to see my reality come to be. An edge, that forced me to pledge, had me recreating another cause and effect.

Handed a whole lot of dead ends. A Hit, run with stagnation in the long run; created a forthcoming event, that served me well. Fast forwarding towards an upcoming dwelling. A new beginning that was meant to be outstanding, ended in failure; for my world turned upside-down without a warning.

Where I saw my reality come to a fold up, for I was told a lie. Purely to serve the corrupts methodology; handing them the energy to feed off the solidarity. I was handed an intensity to clean up and create ostentatious memory. From the old to the new making sure it will lead me through.

Towards the next journey I can relate too. Creating force of events that had me revealing that energy that was haunting me. Handing me the edge relying on that final pledge. Then free myself from you know who. Forcing its way in feeding off the treaty from within.

The drama was over, and I was belittled by he who knew. For the prediction was based on an urge. Admiration to hand the corrupt a chance to hit me with a clarification. Where his mission was to lead me on and to screw me right through. Putting me on a journey, forcing me to remain silent.

I was trapped in a lie, stagnant to my development. A trace that was to be replaced with the old, had brought forth a new beginning. Polishing up on a case, based on a trace I could endeavour to replace. A condition where the clue, created a new atmosphere; burdening the corrupt.

CHAPTER 2

◆ ◆ ◆

FORSEEING A FUTURE EVENT UNFOLD

I was poisoned, with a germ that had me collapse. Where I went after, the energy that caused the effects. It created a force that trapped me in-between. Personally, attacking me had me try my luck; protecting the corrupt. All while trying to harm me and reverse that curse, that come first.

It was challenging he who knew, and those who assumed he could enter my realm. Decided to return then restore their energy and feed off me somehow. Then invade into a my private deedy. Where the troubles, overcome the challenges. It served me well ongoing; in the long run.

A grim response, that was ghastly, had overlapped the energy that failed to respond. It was giving me the choice, I needed to rejoice. A violation to a vibe that forced me to come alive. It handed me the journey that took me on a path that reserved me the right to accommodate another bite.

Where I was given the all clear and a chance to survive one more challenge. Where the journey was misplaced with a trace, that led me towards a pathway; earnest in every way. It forced me to overcome another grimace outcome. Giving me the indication, I was on the road to rejuvenation.

It had me cornered for one more case, a curse I could reverse. All I had to do was accept defeat come first and press delete. Reviving an entrance that was closed when I was hitting the end of the road. An encouragement to a follow up on a key to apply for a trace I could erase.

It was presenting me with a pointless act of kindness. It made my method part of an entertainment; turned me into a visionary handing the corrupt a chance to rely on me in advance. Where time was to serve me well it handed me the key and undid what I thought was part of an evil entrance.

For the world I once knew, was embraced by the old not the new. Where I became energised, by a solution to recreate a journey I can live by. Where I can get in and revolutionise the new beginning. Rebelling against those who knew had me reviewing a viewing; without having to be warned.

I was awarded with a clue, a challenge I did not want to skip. For it was way to juicy, for me, to let go. The corrupt had become interesting, they were on my case watching my every move, assuming I was way too naive to see beyond their glances. The glare was my free ride to accomplish a goal.

Inspiring me to release that feast, had encouraged me to undo another clue. It forced me to reveal the next forthcoming event. The one thing I needed. to retrain my brain and vent. For the interruption was enough for me to witness I was being taught a lesson.

It failed the corrupt, handing me a lead. A given response, towards a journey, that served me well in-between. It was presenting me with a follow up a challenge that was lining me up to carry me towards the journey that served me well and hit me when I hit that forthcoming spell.

I was haunted by the journey, and switched on; by the warning signs. Forcing my way through, was covering up the corrupts final review. It gave me the chance to return in advance; proving I was innocent. I was given a challenge that left me undoing an event, it was returning for a dead-end

It was forming an alliance, leading me towards a journey full of magic. Experiencing magicians, with their own sense of logic. It caved in on me, how personal everything had become. So, when the corrupts journey had me on the edge, it served me well. Well-deserved returning for a hold up.

A hit and run with an amenity, had warned me. For the unjust were on the cast, listing who when and where; just to uncover another keepsake. A trace to that case that was mourning for me to return and release another feast. Where I was given the all clear to return for a final.

It was handing me denial in the long run. A challenge, that forced me to indulge and follow up on a journey. Warning me once again, I was forced to go through hell. Just to give the corrupt a chance to advance and hand me a curse I can reverse. For I was led on, trapped in the middle of a turbulence.

Given an opportunity to clear the air made me eye, those who knew. For they could not wait for me to return and follow up on a journey. Just to screw whatever they assumed will give them the power to return and force their way into my realm. Hitting me with a final entrance.

Demanding an explanation had me on the edge. I on the cusp; living on the edge. Disowning those who pledge, and cursing those who were summoning me to return for unity. I was cornered without a reason, then hit back with; a chamber of illusion. For a deception had me creating a delusion.

It handed me a key, to reunite with those who used me to fight. A separation to my mission, that became part of an evolution. Was preventing me from reliving a final restitution. Evaluating every competition with a partition, it had me questioning the corrupts final improvision.

Handing me a resolution, to challenge the corrupts scepticism; with a repetition. Was encouraging me to return for one more clue, it was to disown the corrupt right through. An everlasting response, had me fishing for information, assuming it was part of an interrogation. An open and shut case.

A test that made no sense to my reality; it had me ceasing the day. I had no chance in hell of challenging it. Because it became part of a game that was revolutionising the energy that created it. Handing me an indication I was hit with a final revelation.

Because the trace was based on a condition, an overwhelming competition. It made several overzealous, serving me well; handing me a forthcoming spell. An outcome, I needed to get through hell. Evaluating every movement, it met me halfway, competing with he who knew.

For he who had a clue, constantly had me on the edge; refining a pledge. Reminding me there is no justice in society. What there was made no sense to my reality. Convincing me otherwise undeniable was nowhere near the corrupts final. My destiny was part of a landslide; to overcome an outcome.

I hit the other side, warned of what was to come next. For I had no chance, of repeating a quest. I had to travel, from one end to the next. Projecting what I assumed, was part of the corrupts final request. An overview of requests, was examined, and the energy that was prominent was the truth.

It had the corrupt rejected, most dependant, on those who served them well then. Back then those who served them were not aware of the outcome; they were lied too. Left to suffer while the rest recover, shocking those who were led to believe, the concept was part of the journey.

In fact, it was part of their greed, where the blame had trapped those who were part of the clue. It became an important role, for those who were part of the lie. living an impatient existence was there way to get by. Waiting for the drama to raid an overdrive, an outcome extended.

An expense to that dread, became part of that expose. It led those who knew, towards my journey. It stated a fact, caused an effect, and burnt out; just before I had a chance to resurrect. Where every past trace had a failed attempt, it caused an effect. Led me to a destination, no more interruption.

My creativity took over, it forced me to resign and start fresh. Where my body collapsed and I felt the energy subside and my spirit subdivide. I had to redo, condition the mission, to my favour. Then teach my whole being, how to relive in a society that harmed me; as I reach my soul purpose.

Cleaning up the mess, left behind on a condition, I speed up the process. For I hit the corrupt with one more admission in mind. A Stagnant effect gave way, it handed me the leeway to accommodate and hit the corrupt with that everlasting trace. A trap to love and hate, while I get back on track.

A follow up on a journey was hinting to the corrupt that their vision was a made-up story. I was nowhere near I was meant to be, because I was served a challenge that was hard for me to accept. It served me unwillingly and handed me a trace, purely to replace that everlasting case.

Catch up, condition what I thought was part of the corrupts mission. Then acclaim, a review and follow up on one more point of view. So, when I reached my peak, I could get to release that demon that forced me to undo another forthcoming clue, without fail, a presence to prevail.

It was leading the corrupt to a destination, that had me restoring another condition. It Forced me to redo and then accomplish another accrue. Just to get back on track and finalise what I thought was part of a trace. A journey I took in vain had failed me then; a given chance to replace the now.

Handing out a better outcome, for the return, would become another dead end. Where yet again without failing another bend; I get to pick up where I left off. All while I manage to get back up revive another hit from where the corrupt left off. Hinting to me what I did to be sent off without a clue.

Following up on a new and improved avenue. Recreated a place in my domain, where I get to release and follow up on a feast. Who were they to return hit me run teach me a lesson on an assumption. Assuming that the method, would not backfire in the long run.

For there was no doubt in mind, the corrupt were two of a kind. Every breath, I took, resembled a challenge that failed me. In the end of that trinity there would be destruction. Hitting an end of that melody, delaying that deception, handing me resurrection a foundation to strengthen.

Leaving me restoring my energy once again, had encouraged the corrupt to surrender. It had them return for a chance to improve that new trace that was pending to be replaced. For the only time I could undo was embrace that case and follow up on a clue; where the corrupt saw me easy,

A challenge for me to enter their realm had me free from anomaly. I could raid their heads confuse them with debts and death threats. Then leave them fighting a lost cause, a clause where they had to surrender and key in the truth, trap me in the middle of a feast then release peace.

Haunting my every move, was the corrupts way of deleting and delaying what they assumed was a grey spot. In fact, it was a death threat that hit me in the end of that delay, it created a piece and forced me to commemorate what I thought was part of my concept.

I was manipulated by the whole concept; it gave me a chance to enhance and light up. The thought was through there were plenty who knew and wanted to use me to get through. But the troubles remained the same, the key, part of a game. A trace that served me well forced me through hell.

It was based on a case, from a past event, hitting the present. It consumed my energy at such an extreme. Where the debt, forced me to please the unjust, leaving me suffering in silence. Warned by the siren, that forced me through hell. Giving me the indication, I was lined up for a final vindication.

It forced me to repeat and failed me to report, a personal vendetta. Purely because, I was to catch up, cleanse what I thought, was part of that dilemma. While I service the corrupt with a dead end, it forced me to pretend, feeding off the mission; preventing the corrupt, from creating a proposition.

A challenge that served me well, at every stagnant approach; was dignified and poignant. I was declined without a good reason, fed a whole lot of lies. Just to get a chance to peak in advance. Fed up with the trauma the decision to return the favour, was an easy way out.

It was a trace to erase that upcoming dilemma. Winning another gamble, was part of the deceit, it was giving me a challenge, forced to repeat. Lined up for a curse I could reverse, was forthcoming. I was fed a handful of lies, where those keys I earned were useless to me.

So, I decided to give in start fresh, free myself from that debt and death threat. Lucky for me I never destroyed the last foundation. I was given a second chance, to prove my innocence in advance. Right at the point where I can return and repeat it. Because in the end the honest truth come to fruition.

I never harmed a living soul, on the purpose to gain stardom; just wisdom. My vision was not impaired, it was part of the game. I had to get through, hit the corrupt with a force, serving me well. I had no fear to enter hell, I was faced holding on to what I thought was upcoming spell.

The test was a quest for me to progress. It was purely to clear my name, hit the corrupt with a final game; return with a vengeance. For I needed to have them surrender, delay no longer, breaking the cycle that was leading me to denial. It was my way to force myself in and hit the corrupt from within.

It had me re-enter and follow up on that everlasting condition. It was part of a competition, where I get in and feed off the industry; that fed off me from within. For I needed repetition, to find common ground. Release inhibition, so I can get back on track, and finalise the competition.

The regret took over the debt, where the deity followed. It handed me freedom, to release my demon, that landed me in a role of fusion. No more competition nor confusion, because I mastered my craft and hit the corrupt with a final trace. Trapping them in the end of the race.

Left stranded, pressured by he who wanted to further. Challenging me in a vendetta, destroying my wellbeing. Assuming hitting me and running, will trap me in the long run. In fact, it gave me a second chance to reflect in my vision. Preventing the corrupt returning for a competition.

I was on the edge restoring what I thought was part of my journey. In fact, it was part of a challenge to get me back on track. It had me stepping into a cathedral full of drama, an ending that was pending. Recreating a journey, I could standby, just to get by; preparing for the next challenge.

Forcing my way through, had me conditioning the mission. I was given an opportunity to return and complete the task, with repetition. A race that led me towards a proposal; was easing my pain. Returning the favour was forcing me to enter the corrupts domain.

A warning, I was nowhere near, completing that task. For the way it was set out, was way over the top. There was no chase to replace, no challenge to trace. It was fake false and misleading; I was led on taught a lesson and left dead to the bone. Warned of what tomorrow may bring forth.

The table had turned long ago; the trace was pointless. There was no key, nor a trick to trap me; just a loyalty card. To reserve the right, to return, hit me back with a follow up on another impact. A challenge to help me proceed had me creating a thirst a quench to come first.

It had me hitting a final a journey; serving me denial. I was stating facts, finalising the impact. While I was stepping into the unknown, it forced me into a world; pausing effects. Where the energy that created the piece, handed me an illusion. Just to return and hit the corrupt with confusion.

Meanwhile handing me a confession had me, lined up for a feast, I could release. All I needed was to come forth and feed off he who knew. Then fast forward to the next final review, the one thought that served me well helped me compel compete and put the corrupt through hell.

I was enlightened with a knowing, part of a wish. It had come to my attention, that the journey was part of the corrupts invention. It failed me, when I hit redemption, for whatever come to fruition handed me the upcoming invasion. Finalising my vision with an interpretation not competition

Just so the corrupt no longer have the opportunity to hit me and run. Finalising the outcome to their favour. For I was hit with a hell forsaken momentum. Where the trace was forthcoming, with an opportunity of life time to hit the corrupt with a final groundwork. A feast just to find peace.

That feast served me well presenting me with a forthcoming spell. It took me on a journey, that handed me an exaltation to that evaluation; towards the next destination. Where the truth caused an effect, presenting with a challenge to recreate a feast. Mislead the next forthcoming release.

What a dangerous thought, that took over; it left me hitting the last resort. It was a pointless act of kindness, that warned me I was about to recreate a forthcoming event. Leaving me haunted by whole concept. For what I thought was part of a resemblance of a past event was half the truth.

The other part was still pending and I was stuck trending. Looking for answers that was helping the corrupt condition the mission and finalise the competition. It was handing me the failure and the force to cause an effect. Presenting the corrupt with an alteration, to a forthcoming evaluation.

CHAPTER 3

◆ ◆ ◆

AN END OF A CURSE I COULD REVERSE WHILE LUCID

A challenge, I had to refine, just to catch up, was finalising my method. It was creating an informative event, it had me releasing my demons. It had forced me to vent. Hitting me with an ending, that was taken by storm. Just to regain, my conscious awareness; against my will again.

All while I return, finalising the end of that trend. It caved in on the concept, by hitting the corrupt with a vengeance. An entrance to the unknown, had given me the impression, I was hitting the end of that depression. While it was presenting me with a key, a challenge had finalised.

It was causing an effect, it had me facing another neglect, just to catch up, get back on track and feed off the corrupt. For my everlasting degree was part of a key, that took over that final review. A melody that served me well, had failed the corrupt; right between heaven and hell.

It gave me a second chance to plummet, finalising that summit. So, when they returned to repeat, the ending will no longer be pending. Because I fell into a vampire effect, those who were in it could not wait to return for another hit and run. It forced me to retaliate and rose above it.

It was giving me every opportunity, to voice my opinion. Handing the corrupt, a dead end to their mission. It forced me to return and hit them with repetition. Where I got in voiced my opinion stepped up a level given into that presentation to revive another interrogation.

I was on the move, healing from the past living in the present. Heading towards the end of what I thought was part of an inner knowing. In fact, it was part of an ongoing event, that turned, into a debt and death threat. Where the pages were burnt and the keys released in the wild.

Without I, in the lead, the game would be useless. It would be touch and go, for all involved; with no warning. Just I, solving that yearning, that was holding me back. For that method was not as scarce it was meant to be. It was part of a reset, an odd momentum that had me holding on to that method.

That method was a trick of the trade, a trap, to delete and delay me. So, I never reach my pinnacle, for I was lead on, left to wonder what the end would be like. Wasting valuable time haunted by the past living in the present and waiting for whatever was meant to come my way.

Eventually realizing when I hit the end of that cycle the beginning of a new one became visible. I was too little too late on the edge, lied to just to be taught a lesson. Then left to return at a later date and press replay, pleasing the corrupts method all the way.

The trace was a given, there was a final challenge; to serve me the truth. It was handing the corrupt an everlasting trace. So, when I hit the end of the race the outcome will work to my favour. I was to continue on my path hitting that wrath and conditioning the mission; knowing I had no competition.

For everything that was meant to come to fruition up to date; The research I did had reached its peak. I took my power back, released that demon that took over. Then took the initiative and forced my way through towards a world I could return traced trap and press replay.

Handing me the challenge, I needed to repeat reflect then face another neglect. Where the energy that took me on that journey forced me to regain then follow up on another game. I got to see my light shine independently; handing me the entrance to the unknown.

It was causing the effects; it turned everything upside down. Then it prepared me for a new crown. It faced me, head on, when the journey became easy. It was handling the drama in leaps and bounds, leading me towards the dream independently; about to redeem another theme.

I was on the move, trying my luck to improve. Only to witness my journey was undone. The only case left, was the one that hunted me down and starved me of affection. So, when I hit the end of that redemption. The key that was failing me caved in on the concept; presenting me with an award.

While I was trapped in the middle of a trace, the case become unwilling. It had sacrificed the journey and handed me the trace; it landed me a role that served me well in the end of the race. It gave the corrupt a chance to hit me in advance, warning me; the journey was part of a universal law.

It laid a foundation around the system. Where I get in and finalise that win fighting the system; independently from within. A self-governing state of mind, took me on a journey of discovery. It had me come first, relying on no one thought; the last resort. A challenge that had me undoing a screw.

I was forced to restore the energy, that gave me the power to save my soul. It hit the corrupt, feeding off them whole. For he who served me well then, faced me now. It gave me a challenge forcing me to wind up a trace. When I hit the end of the race, the case closed;

ending in my favour.

Failing the corrupt, right before they hit an encore was enough for me to witness, an interruption. A force to cause the effects. It hit me just before the corrupt haunted me with an encore. For I ran the risk of hitting that feast, that forced me to release; about fail me at every feast.

I was handed an opportunity, to scrutinize the corrupts methodology. It left the case closed, and I damn straightening out clearing the debt, trying to get out. Trapped in the middle of a chaos, tracing the wrong faith chasing the wrong dream, releasing that demon in-between.

For the reality that enforced me to embrace a case, handed the corrupt opportunity to give in. It forced its way in, then encouraged me to hand them a return to evolve and hint another overload. It forced them to recreate a foundation that handed me the melody to revive another dive.

All while I entertain them with the uncertainty. For what tomorrow will bring to the surface, only time will tell. All I know is the corrupt are about to walk into my Dynasty; unwelcome. Where they are about to be put through hell. The only way out will be the way in no meaning no win.

Just a failed attempt on their end and lucky dip and win on mine. For they were not to enter my realm they were not to cross boundary one false move and I will cause an effect and hit them with a curse they cannot reverse because I come first and they need me to get in and I am not giving in.

AMEN

The journey they chose, to involve me in, was a terrible lie. I was used and abused purely to get by. They made up stories in my head, trying to convict then convince me otherwise. It trapped me and left me returning to harmonise; the next of kin. Just so I can get in and feed off the trap from within.

What a challenge I was on, where the adventure to keep strong was ongoing. It was beginning to look extensive. An expense that lasted for a minimal amount of time, long enough to hit me run and finalise that ever-coming outcome. An effect that forced me to catch up and hit the corrupt.

For the ending that was pending became part of a challenge that was never ending. It violated the path that hit me when I hit the end of that wrath. They were feeding of the key that forced me to repeat another case. It had me on the edge, finalising that extended tread.

A contract, that had been facing me was ending in fear. The journey in itself, had no faith nor chase. All it had was a given to hand me the reason to restore my energy and feed off the vision. For I was on the edge a pathway to a journey where I was handed a clue.

It gave me a second chance to review and follow up on a challenge, I cannot deny. Because the corrupt had no time out nor a trace to force me to get by. It presented with another pledge hitting the end of that method. Where I give in and feed off the trauma from within.

It warned me of the cause, that forced me to finalise the end of that remorse. It forced me to redo and follow up on a forthcoming clue. Treating me as if I never knew holding me hostage at every silent review. That is when I knew I was given the end of one trap and handed another trace.

When I hit the end of my tither, the energy that served me well then, was to shrivel up and wither. For what was to come next, had no rhythm, just a request, to follow up on a test. Handing me the trend I needed to return and pretend. For I was on the move hitting the end of that groove.

It reserved me the right, to accommodate on another fight. Ease my pain, refrain me from going insane. Just to release that feast, that served me well, when trapped in hell. It gave me a chance to develop my intuition in advance. So, when I hit the end of my trace the condition will be replaced.

Where I see the light fight, that everlasting bight. So, when I hit the end of my trace, the beginning will be replaced. I will hit an entrance to the unknown. warning the corrupt there was no way they were going to re-enter and press replay; form the old. It was time to start new a space in-between.

For I always knew, I was to be used, abused then left to suffer. A test for me to be able to live in somewhat peace; no longer lie to myself. For the journey, was based on a case to harm those who interrogate and follow up on another vision. It served me well, and put me through.

It was forcing me to return for vendetta. I was set up by those who knew; I call the corrupt. They were on my case, hiding in the corner, waiting to catch up. Little did I know at the time, several were on my trace, parking in places they thought they were not visible to my peripheral vision.

In reality, I was trapped, trying to find the way out, just to catch them in the act. Handing out a sense of doubt; was the only way I could face another day. For I was being watched; I had a knowing too, it forced me to repeat take that trap and wrap it up following up on another clue.

The revelation to that divination, was justifying the corrupts final admission. It had me finalising that attentive reflection, pausing effects, and handing me the end of that deception with one more upcoming event, it forced me to return for repetition. Warning me I hit the end of that mission.

It had me examining every thought, terrorising the corrupt while stating a fact. It forced me to wrap it all up and push the corrupt off track. It was handing them an outcome that will serve me well an upcoming event that will push the corrupt off their limits again.

Waiting for the right time to hit me three-fold. Wondering into the unknown was presenting me with a gnome. A short stumpy character who wore shades to cover his thoughts returning to Serve me well. A sentence towards a final interaction, about to achieve another spell.

Every time I hit that forthcoming trace. It trapped the corrupt and served me a challenge, I could embrace. The energy that trapped me then, fed off me now. Meeting that gnome landed me a role. It handed me the energy to feed and follow up on a new journey.

It was purely for me to return, succeed. Then enter the unknown, with the energy that had me waiting patiently to engrave my name in the middle of my domain. For I needed to endow then release that piece to the unknown. So, when I reached my peak, I was forced to delete.

Start fresh, hit the day I went public, so when I reached my peak. The only challenge I had left was the one that hit me with a lie; just so the corrupt can get by. It was failing me at every proposal it had me tied down left me producing an energy that was harming me.

It warned me once again, where the only test I was given, was the one that served me well. It handed me the forbidden. Where the energy that faced me presented with a clue, it forced me to eradicate a point of view. An ending that was pending and a beginning that was never ending.

All while I was forced to hit the corrupt with remorse, serving them well. A trace I could not replace. It forced me to turn against those who I thought were part of a world-wide catastrophe. In fact, it was a joke from the start, and those who knew could not wait to make me think otherwise.

That made up story in my head, no longer fascinated me. Nor did it fail me, when I hit the end of that trend, I was handed a clue it had me forced to return for remorse. Caving in on the concept and making sure, when I hit the end of that trace; the made-up story in my head will be replaced.

It will harm those who harmed me to get ahead. Test the patience of those who were summoning me for attention haunting me with redemption. Hoping I will give in handing them confirmation. For that Dead end, and death threat will pass. I will release that feast that forced me to find peace.

For I was given the all clear, a chase to erase that final case. Where the corrupt were to enter my realm and finalise it to my favour with no doubt or made-up story in my mind to keep me quiet and them alive. A chance to hit them in advance was inevitable, it was my way of stating a fact.

A challenge, that served me well presented me with a forthcoming spell. It led me to believe the lie was true and I was on the edge presenting the corrupt with a final pledge. It was purely to catch up and finalise the end of that trend that served me well and forced me through hell.

For that deep and meaningful response, became a chaotic effect. It hit me when I hit a dead end, warning me to release that piece, then force my way in, just to a way it down. Then have me enter the corrupts realm, lining me up for another hit and run.

A conspiracy that took over my journey, was validated. It had been raised above and beyond for a long-term effect. Where in the end the trace had been pending and the drama never ending. It caused an effect and presented me with a clue. It gave me the free ride to follow up on an overview.

It had come to my attention that the corrupt were revealing another competition. It became a final feast that served me well and hit me with a forthcoming spell. It forced me to return for another cause and effect. It had become unprecedented that the end of that trend was burning me.

I was on the edge, protecting my soul, warning my spirit I was about to walk into a mission wholistically. All while I accomplish another competition, waiting for the concept to roam. Before I fell into that role, that was forcing me to feed off that journey wholistically.

Given a challenge, that was releasing a piece of my destiny, to early. It caused an effect and left me hitting the end of that trend, handing it to another handing them a chance to further. It was part of the invasion that was serving me a fusion, to that conclusion.

It gave the corrupt a chance, to hit me run and deceive me in the long run. I had no choice, but to present the corrupt with an illusion. It had me living in on the edge releasing a feast, adding to their confusion. Mourning for the corrupt at every delusion, was an expense less likely for me to restore.

A task that brought me a challenge I did not ask for, it had me feeding off the concept. It was way too hard to ignore, ignite or even fight, it was part of a feast that warned me; time to release. Presenting me with chaos every time I hit the end of that presentation.

Forcing me to feed of that confirmation, was delightful. It taught me a lesson to help me reach my potential. Relying on no one to get through saved me and handed me the progression to conspire too. Hitting the corrupt with confusion, a condition that hit me when I hit the end of that position.

Just so I can feed off the revelation, it handed me the destination I needed to refine and reform to the next presentation. It was delaying and deleting the corrupt mental; leaving them irrational. handing me a breakthrough conditioning the mission to my confusing me when I hit the final degree.

It had me, hunting for feast, stirring the pot, on the condition; I return for repetition. All while I was on lease, about to release peace. Presenting the corrupt with several chances to hit me, then run assuming that will kill me. Only to witness there was no competition in my mission.

Because I completed my task and competed with the wrong people. The journey I was on had no chance in hell, of repeating without a fight. It was based on a constant reminder and repetition, to hand me no competition. Just constant conviction to deal the mission and hand me a proposal.

With no vision, nor trace to compel, I was left to live in hell. Haunted by the past, living in the present no chance in hell of failing another competition. Because the trace was part of a case that handed me a clue. It gave me the energy and the power to push through.

CHAPTER 4

◆ ◆ ◆

HOW EVERY FIGHT BECAME AN ABSOLUTE DELIGHT

Not only I made it, to where I was meant to be; quite interestingly. I had others trying their luck, to finalise the mission and hand me bad luck. Assuming I was a victim to their scrutiny; a pointless affair. Where I entered on a condition; I win every mission. No doubt in my mind, I hit the divine.

The method that I once knew, was based on a clue. It served me well and presented me with a forthcoming spell. It handed me the result I needed to undo, and create a final overview. For what I thought was an ongoing analysis, became part of a journey that mentally praised me.

It took a turn for the better, a final request, for the test to compress. For I was to return to be handed a key that cave in on my road and was meant to be part of my destiny. It was an entrance to the unknown, that created the oblivion. It was to trace that trapped me and served me well.

For I was in it to win it, and the challenge I was handed, was no longer branded. It had me forced to encounter another trace to that case. Turning the atmosphere towards a general trace. It forced me to redo and repair, whatever was needed to be fixed. For the journey was never part of that twist.

It served me well, failing their method every step of the way. It was the only way I could prepare myself towards with a journey I could relate to. For every thought that came to mind, was part of a trace that was trapping me in the end of the divine. An endeavour to move on with the times.

Where I get in, trace trap and win; giving the corrupt grief from within. Where I never lose control just finalise that piece that forced me to release. It was to follow up on a case personally attacking those who encourage me to erase. While I continue to embrace a condition to replace the mission.

No longer following up on another competition. For it served me well and handed me a forthcoming spell. Because what I thought I knew was partially a trace to repeat and replace. Giving me the indication I hit the end of civilization, for it was the vendetta that created the war.

It had me on the other end, living vicariously, ceasing to wonder. When will the corrupt stop pretending. Creating a war in my peace using methods to create a war hit me and run and finalise that upcoming event once more. It forced me to wean, everything I knew.

For what it was worth, there was no value, just a timeout, added with a testimonial. An approval from the other end, was a given and I had reached my peak. Where the only challenge left was the one where I was stabbed by those who were trying to befriend me; the true enemy.

When I hit the forbidden, I could undo; restore my energy. A warning, to hand down what I thought was a hunt down. In fact, it was a run down, then a countdown, to repeat another show down. A chance in advance to witness first hand; who is in on it, and who had the energy to state it.

Where I get in, reveal the corrupts proposal from within. For I was given an opportunity to delve into another scrutiny. Meanwhile drop that bomb, a trace that served me well. Handing me the entrance to that upcoming spell. It was to warn the corrupt to keep out and no longer return.

I lost my way, forced to play it the corrupts way. Told to wait for them to write a wrong then try my hardest to remain strong. As if they knew I was returning to create a new yearning. Instead of going with the plan they killed it attempting to kill me and my spirit; adding to my problem.

I was way ahead of them, and the plan to harm me again was backfiring. It was forcing me to relive and affiliate with those who knew and wanted me to fail; so, I never prevail. It was preventing me from living the unholy grail. It forced me to repeat and follow up on a trace.

The one incurable case, it had me facing another trend. It was finalising the energy that forced me to pretend where in the end I gave in and decided to rewrite the destination of he who rewrote mine on the condition I feed off him contaminate their soul from within.

It had me feeding off the path, that was returning for a yearning. It was a case I could erase a challenge that forced me to meddle in the affairs of those who revive. I had no idea it was part of a trend that faced me in the middle of an upcoming riddle.

I was to repeat, repel and comprehend; what end will save me in the end. It was part of a trace that was pending and a curse that was mending, every momentum. It was withstanding the pain of the end of that game it took me in and gambled that trace that forced me to erase that case.

Saving the corrupt, handed me a method that was erupt. It was part of a trace that was pending. Handing me the indication I was reserved another observation. So, I decided to give in return and belt the corrupt from within. Desiring the one key that forced me to reveal that upcoming event.

A trace to trap me in the end, leading me towards a violent attack. It made the corrupt stagnant defiant, about to start a riot. Trying to defend their honour had them losing a battle. Because they played it dirty the trace was erased and the key that was stolen from me was handed to me freely.

No strings attached, no time to return and respond with an attack; because I hit the ether. I went so far up, towards the heavens, I could see the light. Grounding me here was hard I could not respond because I was left shameless. For the energy that faced me then hit me twice as hard now.

It was a trace that trapped me in the middle of a praise. Bruising every precious moment, had become a cunning response to validate the next troubled mission. For every preparation had a momentum. I was on the edge stating facts retaliating at every tread.

All while I wait for the right moment to pledge. Conditioning the mission and validating another competition. Handing me a clue and trapping those who knew. Purely to step in then take a moment to step back then finalise what I thought was part of a journey I could review.

A given challenge to restore my energy, served me a condition I could not refuse. It was purely to recreate a vendetta, I could relate too, I was forced to return and give the corrupt a chance to remain vigilant. It was part of a challenge that had them entering a final quest.

I was hitting a question mark, a challenge that was causing an effect. It handed me a warning, a reoccurrence to a dead end. I was treading for a first and last faith. It was less likely to erase an everlasting thought to that trace. It served me well at the end of that forthcoming event.

Where I cast a spell, by chanting their name. Then engraving it, in the middle of the corrupts final remains. Finalising those turn of event was turning the key, jinxing he who tried to put a hex on me. Then Lock them in, revealing another debt to that threat it forced me to reveal an upcoming event.

While I conspire to hit them from within. Holding them hostage as I condition the mission, was parting and the vision changed. I was handed a key, a clue to finalise that feast it was trapping the corrupt in the middle. It was returning at every yearning handing me a final retrieval.

Where the rest hit denial, and I on the edge had returned for a yearning. Where I had to play it the way it was written, then when the time come; hit the forbidden. Troubling that method was pointless, it had me enforcing a hit. It caused an effect and finalised that debt.

I was on the move, restoring my energy; finalising the truth. It gave me the ending, that was pending a hunt down that was never ending. A remorseful event, it was hitting me with a faith less likely for me to succumb, from a failed outcome. I was to retrieve a key and trap those who violated me.

It was part of a curse that I could not reverse. Unless I rewarded the corrupt with a key. The journey backfired it handed me a duty of care, and a challenge that forced me to recreate another test. A trace I had to compel compete and finalise another trend, to that bend, that hit me in the end.

In case that position hit me to early, I had to end the race sooner. Feeding off the trace and restoring my energy at every case. For the competition forced me to recreate a journey I could relate to. There would be no vice to detest or a case to contest. Because the journey had become a request to untie.

For every clue was a shade of grey, hovering over those terms and conditions. For those who press replay, were given permission to return for a competition. It was part of a curse, I could not revue, revive nor even hit the edge, without fighting a lost cause.

For this time around, time was of essence and I was running out of time. I was warned of the outcome given a chance to reveal and revive another trend to that bend that forced me to take control and hit the corrupt in the end. For I was no longer spared, wasted, or even compared.

For the corrupt were fighting a lost cause, a heroic method, that had me torn into shreds. It stripped me of my dignity and the energy that served me well was harming me in the end. For those who were sacrificing my soul hade me on the edge warning them once again.

Where this time I am happy for them, not only do I wish them well. But the end result handed them a challenge with a service, resulting to where the stratagem will state a fact. Handing out the end of that trend, so I can get back on track, feeding of those who release a feast.

Forcing me to double take, had become a challenge; beyond doubt. Allowing no uncertainty to take over that adversity. I got in, took a sneak peak, then lined the corrupt up for one more cheat sheet. A chance to stir the pot, hit a trace in advance, then take that trend forcing me to embrace a case.

All so I can return hit them in advance, revealing what I knew all along. I was way off tap, trapped in the middle of thirst so I can come first. Rewarding those who did not deserve it. Warned of a trace that forced me to recreate a curse, just to reverse. It was a Given foundation to come first.

A condition, that had been repeating an old wound, was a given. It was part of a past event, that handed me the challenge that was no longer forbidden. Once bitten twice shy, had handed me the outcome, to encourage me to recreate a challenge; serving me well in the long run.

Presented with a key, had forced me to get through, that virtual reality. Without failing a clue, I was given a final review, a chance to look forward and feed off the edge. No entrance for the corrupts return for a threat. It was based on a case that was blocked, encouraging me to hit run then calve.

I had no recollection, of a test that was meant to harm me at the end of that request. I found myself in a position disrupting the corrupts final redemption. It led me to a debt collection, a challenge to save me when I hit the end of that catastrophic event.

Where I get in click collect everything, then start fresh. Handing the corrupt a dead end to that threat. Freeing myself from a coverup, where the corrupt were about to Telly up the scores. Then delegate hit me with a force that will serve me at the end of that course.

It was part of a breed, a past dilemma that left me hunting the corrupt down; for another vendetta. A waste of energy, was forming it was handing me a key; starving of industry. For I hit a hidden talent, a repeat to condition the mission and follow up on another competition.

A made-up story in my head, was restoring my energy to make it easy. A regretful event, had stated a fact, it gave me a trace to get back on track. I had to track down those who used me to get in. Assuming their reality will over power mine, an indication they could hit me one day at a time.

When the pot was hot, they could stir as many times as they want. Simmering slowly, not allowing it to burn out, nor evaporate as yet. A reality check had become part of that debt. For they assumed, an opportunity arose, favouring that threat. Handing me the edge I needed to reclaim another debt.

I was hit with scrutiny; a knot tied so tight, only the

urge to splurge will undo that clue. It forced me to redo another validation to that foundation. Hoping it will suffocate the energy that failed me. It warned me I hit the end of that trend that was stirring me.

Hoping the energy that hunted me down, will cut that trace, in half. It tracked me down and handed me the evaluation to cave in on the concept. It fed off the one thing that had me warned I was hitting an ending from within. Cutting the corrupts method into portions.

I was given a faith to be reckoned with, a curse to reverse. Where the challenge will come first. I was handed an ending that was pending, a faith that was never-ending. It forced me to pretend there was no trace in the end. Just to have me make up another story in the head.

Wording it their way, was no way to live. I had to repeat, report, then leave it to chance. Lying to myself so the corrupt can advance then continue while I live in doubt. A threat that served me well. While the rest clean up the mess. Just so they can get ahead; holding me hostage all the way.

It was hitting an ending, where the entrance was pending. A trace that was never ending, turned into a nightmare. It had become part of the corrupts vengeance, pursued, hijacked then lined up for a cover up. It had me bathing in the corrupts filth, dirtying my spirit; there way of emancipating.

I was not flattered nor was I conditioning the mission to hand the corrupt a competition. For, there were several who wanted a piece of the action. I was trapped traced followed up by an abreaction, just to complicate things. A compliment to the corrupts final entrapment, handing me the edge.

The reason was based on a case, that was caving in on the lie. I had no energy to reveal the truth, nor did I want to waste valuable time facing the corrupt and handing them another chance to get by. I was warned, I had no freedom to undo nor review what I had was to reveal a case to that trace.

I was held hostage it had me facing the truth. What I had was enforcing the corrupt to come forth. It forced me to erase a condition, then release all inhibition, a mission accomplished a trace that was hitting the edge handed me a case that forced me to anticipate another final.

Where the journey had given me a challenge, that served me well. It gave me a chance to deliver that second trial the one that forced off the edge straight into a positive light. It was a hit that forced me to review and follow up on another encounter with the corrupts final endeavour.

It presented me with a clue, it handed me another point of view. So, when I reached my peak the energy that served me well, forced me to entrap those who knew Where they decided to make me out to be there victim. Scrutinising me thoroughly was encountering an edge; a touch of regret.

Looking for ways to repeat and hit every step of the

way was hounding the corrupt all the way. The thought they could hit me run with unity took the edge out of me. It made me hurry it all up just to give the corrupt a chance to tally up, then hit the corrupt with denial now.

What a challenge I had to reveal just to siege an encounter. A force to that cause that was failing me every time I hit the end of that mediocre. A platonic momentum that forced me to reveal a competition was surreal. It was giving me the end of that trend and the beginning of a final.

A meeting with a trial and an error, failed me after that vendetta. For when I hit the end of that trend, it was encouraging the corrupt to return and hit me again. Letting them in after the fact would cause an effect and hand me a trace to get back on track.

It was presenting me with a deliberation a trace that will force me to review. A given clue, that gave me the dedication, I needed to survive on air. Delivering a fact with an encouragement to get back on track. An encounter with whom where the troubles took the corrupt on a journey.

A challenge that delivered that sermon; passed that fake intake. Interrogating a trace that forced me to release that feast. Warning me the path I was on, had no clearance for the corrupt to remain strong. It forced me to review cause and effect, handing me the knowledge to recreate a dead end.

CHAPTER 5

◆ ◆ ◆

AN ACCOMPLISHED JOURNEY HITTING A VOID

A threat that failed me then, took me on now. It had me returning, to restore my energy somehow. I was back on track, repeating an old passageway. A hell forsaken momentum, terrorising those who were rising above the intention. For it was the invention that handed me the outcome.

The intention had no validation, nor did it have a concept to meet me halfway. It was part of a force to repeat another bad day. It had served me a nest full of hope, it had me pass tests then return to regress while the rest progress. It failed me when I hit a development, serving me entertainment.

It was part of a present attack a task, that handed me a red flag. A regret, to restore my energy from the past and start fresh. It was part of a challenge that handed me a clue, an accrue; just to create a better avenue. So, when the time come, I could free myself for a challenge that hit an ending.

Part of a challenge, that was pending for a while gave me the know-how. It showed me how to survive another dive. A conclusion, served me an ending that hit the raw. There was no challenge to relate to nor a trace to condition to replace. A warning the outcome was mine for the taking.

I was served a challenge, more than I could handle. It lined me up for a clue, finalising that everlasting review. Feeding off those who knew caved in on me. It restored my energy and refused the corrupt entrance. A chance to return in advance, all while attempting to accomplish a goal.

Assuming they could swindle their way in. Took me on a journey lining the corrupt up for a win. A trace I could replace, a trace that had taken its toll. I was on the edge repeating another role It served me well and forced me to feed off the corrupt whole.

A challenge I had no chance of restoring, had come and gone. I was left waiting for a lost cause to come to fruition. Then undo what the corrupt were planning to do after the fact, for that was the mission. Before they had me hitting the end of that edge that was forcing me to repeat.

It gave me an entrance, sweetening the deal. I hit the corrupt, just before I hit an encore. It had me pledging for what I thought was part of a trend. In fact, it was a test to trick and treat the corrupt as an enemy and hand them a dead end. Just so I can return and repeat another rude awakening.

It served me well; it handed me a forthcoming spell. The entrance I needed to condition the mission had presented me with a vision. A preparation to harm the corrupt at every reservation. It had me lined up for one more condition; confirming the obvious.

I had no time out, nor freedom to scheme. A theme brought me forward, before I had a chance to undo that clue. For he who took control of me, had my destiny, on edge. Raiding the heads of others. Handing an opportunity to join; a plot. A stalker to inform them the game; a gamble to aim.

For what it was worth, a belief, that I was part of that union; was just a train of thought. The corrupt entered my realm, tampered with my vision, and attacked my intuition. Leading them on and making them think they were on the right track. It was the only way for me to get back on track.

I had no choice, I had to rejoice, follow up on another vision. Side track, their train of thoughts, all by undoing a knot that had attached to my spirit. Attacking the edge, ride to the other side, that had me about to spray venom. It had me spread a rumour to get in; sacrifice the corrupt from within.

A rude awakening, that was up and going had me on the edge. It was presenting the corrupt with another pledge. Where they handed me the freedom to hit me and run; back when. Giving me the opportunity to see how they play it so I can return and hit them threefold.

Then return yet again and keep hitting them until I reach my threshold. I had no freedom to fight back; back then. Because my chances were minimal, I had no foundation my light was bright but the edge I was handed was turning heads handing me the loss added with gain to confuse me again.

I had already lived it and lost the first battle. The second one was a trap, somewhat a breeze; for I had to fight back, by testing the corrupts patience. That was the only way I could succeed. So, when I reached my peak, I could feed off the clue make it to the end and start again. Fresh off the boat.

A battle that led me on, gave me hope; then failed me, in the long run. For a strange habit, arose form a past concept. It caused an effect and an energy that left me returning for another yearning. It kept repeating itself and I kept strung and hung along with same old melody.

Whatever came to fruition, had hit a boundary, it was setting me up for a fall. If I did not fight back, I would lose it all. It was handing me the same proposition, a game that had me on the edge gambling it all away. I once again, on a mission trying to hit back with the same stupid vision.

It was lining me up, for a case I could not erase. For it was part, of an ending that was hinting to me I hit the oblivion. An obvious task, where the vision was interpreting a challenge. It served me well and handed me a forthcoming spell. I had no recollection, because from corrupts final redemption.

I was released, then trapped once again, in the middle of a feast. Reserving the right to come to terms with the fact I was on the edge. It had me returning for a new improved pledge. A challenge that handed me the reasoning, just to return for one more reckoning.

A given a moment was about to flow, where each challenge had a boost of energy. I on the edge returning for one more plea. That was to have the corrupt plead guilty. For I was given the all clear, and a presentation to evaluate another truth to that flawless event that handed me content.

I had to outdo the corrupts final review, then project it to my favour, so I can feed off that too. Then look forward to the rest, catchup and feed off that next contest. It was a given, I was to challenge the corrupt to the next provision. A competition I could confront, heading for a trace I could erase.

They made me a runner up, to a competition that was not handed to me properly. They served me well, handed me everything on a silver platter just so I give in. The wool over my eyes had covered with more than I could handle. The drama took over and the trace became a scandal.

Just so they can win another inning, trapping me with a challenge that had me on the edge. Responding to the corrupts mission, was leading me to a destination that handed me a final competition. Not only I was served a dream but they handed me a lot failure in between.

A need to close one gate, and open another, was up to date. They knew that I was on the move, and they tried to distract me so I never get through. What a trace I had to embrace just to get back on track and condition the mission. I was given a competition forced in admission then handed a vision.

I was casing another trend, feeding off what I thought, was the last resort. Ceasing to wonder; who what when and how it will end, was a trace I had to reverse to come first. Purely on the edge waiting for the corrupt to return and pledge. Returning for one more hit then heave at the outcome.

It had me causing effects, waiting for the challenge to resurrect. It gave me a second chance to trace, trap and cover up another attempt. For those who restored their energy by feeding off mine. Had no case to erase just a challenge to present with a key. Finalising the verdict that was haunting me.

For the energy that served me well then, was no longer part of the trend. It was purely to let go of a warning, for the corrupts method was not as incredibly strong as I assumed. To be honest I hit the end, and the curse was about to be reversed. Handing me the second trail, just to come first.

Trapping those who pretend, was giving me the outcome I needed to trap them again. Where this time around I get to pretend and laugh at them just to catch up and follow up on another challenge again. I was forced to keep up with the program, just to cancel out the two.

It was part of a past trace, where the clue turned into a nasty revenue. I was left struggling, handing me an ending that was pending. It took me on a journey where I had to piece it all together one by one; like a jigsaw puzzle. There were pieces scattered in every direction, reminiscing a past event.

It was part of an extended warranty, a foundation that hunted me down. It was lining me up for another crown of glory. On the edge, pleasing those who had me rising above and beyond the wrong the right and the extended warranty a case I had no chance in hell of repeating.

It was a given, a replacement of a key, trapped in the middle of a condition. Haunting me with repetition. I was hyped up, with a thought, it hit me when I hit the corrupt. Lining me up for a competition, on the edge, restoring another vision. Presenting me with an entourage.

Waiting to survive a dive, had me questioning, the motivation of those who survived. It left me warned, living on the edge, stepping into the unknown. A stepping stone to the next level. Wondering when where and who were stirring trouble. Creating a free enterprise to those who hit.

For they were given an advantage and I was left to suffer in silence. Watching them face me then fail me while they were handing me a trace I could not embrace. It was part of an accordance to a trace that served me well at the end of the race. For a certain rule changed the way I witnessed the world.

Where the challenges that served me well then, had forced me to undo a forthcoming clue. For I was given a disadvantage, it had lined me up for a challenge that served me with a vengeance. It was well thought by those who were encouraged to use abuse and throw me out.

It hit me just before, I was handed an encore. For I was on the brink of causing an effect, it had released a presentation. For I was on the edge of every reservation proposing another composition to that mission. It was restoring my energy and facing another case to that trace.

It had me presented with one more task; purely to terrorise the corrupt at last. Forcing my way in and creating a war in the corrupts mission so I can continue to reap a reward was nowhere near the personal vendetta. It forced me to come forth handing out another resort to that cause and effect.

I was being served well, reaching a point of no return. Holding on to a past influence, was my way of returning the favour; I had experience. It was restoring my energy at every significance. Hurrying up was no way to please the corrupt either. It forced me to word it my way; through the highway.

An option that served me well, opted out freely. Where I was given a challenge that forced me to redo that final review. Back where I started reviewing another clue, only to witness the corrupt had it in for me and the only way for me to get through was take that warning and walk away.

Starving the corrupt of affection, while I reach that final redemption; was part of a cover up. It was purely to undo that final review, it hit me when I hit the end of that melody. It was giving me the impression the power to redo a spell will serve me a case to be erased; handing me the edge.

It forced me to hit run and finalise the power of trinity; within my vicinity. Validating what I knew and what trace will hand me the outcome to overcome that trick that me on a ride towards the light. It was to reveal what I thought was the truth. In fact, it was another lie for the corrupt to get by.

I was hit with a condition, that forced me off the edge. It was handing me a composition, that was proposing a vile competition. It had me on the edge proposing what I thought was part of a valid response. Giving me the indication the trace was part of a tread that handed me the case.

Purely to reveal, revive, catch a break, catch up. Then create a case, I could embrace. All while I give in to that method that was restoring the one thing that weighed me down. When I hit the end of that trend it had me relying on what I thought was part of last resort.

It caught me by surprise, a challenge that forced me to redo and accomplish another clue. It gave me a second chance to return; hitting the corrupt in advance. Just so when I catch up, I get in challenging the corrupt; where I win every inning. Hitting them all while I interrogate them.

It was part of an edge, waiting for the corrupt to return reappeal. While I am presented with a final reveal. It handed me a revelation, to work in unison, with those whom were deserving. It turned me into an oblivion idiot. Warning me the only way in was the way out; even then, there was no doubt.

It handed me a key, purely to reveal, an edge; a part of my pavilion that was causing effects. Having me cleanse a challenge that was on the brink of collapsing. Was acclaimed by a thread it hit me in the end. It was handing me a new tread, forcing me to deal with a key; I could not rely on or reveal.

I was too busy trying to step into an entrance, that was haunting me. It was taking its time, and surprising me with an extra vine. Creeping up on me at every level so when I reached my peak the energy that salvaged that trend handed me the level of abundance that failed me in the end.

I was on another level, contradicting those who were trying their luck. For I stepping forward, was handing them bad luck. I could sense another hit and run about to overcome the corrupts outcome. Presenting me with one more key, a cancelation to that treasure a long-term effect.

A challenge I could handle, was infinite, it was restoring my energy. Handing me the silence, whenever I needed to complete a task. Just so I can return and clean the mess that was left behind. For the concept that took me on that journey was serving me well.

The reason being, I was on that track, an indication, I had reserved. It handed me the right to accommodate another fight. It created a treason, to that journey that handed me victory, so when I reached the finish line, I hit the corrupt first and last. Leaving nothing to the imagination behind.

It was part of a concept, an illusion to hand out confusion. I had tracked down the energy that had me focused on a journey that was stalling; it forced me to be cautious. A conclusion that had me convinced that the corrupt were on the edge, trapped ready to clear the debt.

A hint of deception, handed me the energy that I needed to return, for redemption. An ending that was based on a condition, warned me of the fake and false opposition. It had me on the edge revealing the corrupts final admiration. For I was in the middle of an upcoming event.

It was brought to my attention that the game was based on a past case. It had handed me redemption and a follow up to the next destination a distinction to that confirmation that took me on a run and fed off the energy that served me well in the long run.

A given challenge that kicked a fuss, put me on a journey that lit up. It created a lineup of affairs. A case that served me well and presented me with a phase. It had me on the edge, Presenting the corrupt with a challenge they could not be erased. Putting me on a path that served me well.

It tracked the corrupt down, freed me from a crowd of cowards. For they were trying there hardest to harvest. Lining up at my doorstep proving to me they were clearly on the edge; stalking me. Hitting me every time they were told too. Where they took me in forced me to lose, an advantage.

A gamble that forced me to revive another dive from within. It had me returning for one more yearning. A trace that forced me to get in and replace that upcoming event. It was lining me up for a feast I could undo release and feed off the vision that handed me a competition.

It was serving me well and presented me with an upcoming spell. Where I had given in presentation that led me towards a foundation that forced me to release that upcoming feast. Failing those who overcome and feed off the end of that trend that lined me up for a new improved journey.

A game that took me in overlapped; serving me well from within. As I hit the end of that trend, the events that followed will work to my favour. It lined me up for a case that hit the corrupt at the end of the race. Harming those who assumed, luring me in; will give them the power to win. No kidding!

CHAPTER 6

◆ ◆ ◆

WHEN I MEET THE CORRUPTS TWIN & I'M PEAKING

I had to follow-up on a dream, scheme in between. Hold the corrupt up; keeping the drama pending. An injustice had peaked, it was parting ways from the drama. Entering the unknown, repeat that debt with ease. Then hit the corrupt right between delete delay; leading them astray all the way.

It was part of an expose; it led me near a leeway. An opening to a passageway towards the pantheon. Enough, to hold the forte, proving my innocence. It started a fight, lined me up for a win, then pressed against the will, of those who had skill. I had to think twice, at every upcoming event.

For every time I hit a trace the personal vendetta would overcome the tremor. I would be back where I started, undeniably on the mend. Presenting me with a key that had troubled me when I hit the end. Because the key I earned was stolen, and I had to rebuild and start again.

I was on my path, admiring what the future may hold. Creating a piece, that will remain somewhat vigilant to the game. Where I could sustain, then release peace. All by covering up that game then gambling the one thing that served me willingly from within.

For the gate remained solid, wide open; purely so I can get in. Releasing the demons from within, finalising that trend, forming a new improved theme. So, when I hit that scheme, the journey I once knew will trouble those who condition every mission to their saviour; stirring every raider.

Assuming they had the power to return the favour. Lining me up for a key that was purely feeding off me. For I was on the edge returning to devour, a faith less likely to breath. In fact, I had the corrupt shocked to the system. Cornered so I can achieve a goal and back on track.

I was on the move; waiting patiently for the corrupt to return in the foreseeable future. Luck on my side and one thought to override was giving me the power to revive and survive another conniving act of kindness. I witnessed first-hand the return was a percentage of no return.

Handing them a key to tranquillity, an assumption

that is a joke to me. In return, there is no such luck in humanity. If you want to live in this world, you must suffer and try your luck. Because the world is surrounded by individuals who want what you have; not the best because, it is a test.

They will go to such extents, to harm you, so you never get there. Where they strike with a vengeance, hit you when you reach your temperance. Attempt to mind read you, a skill that many have and like to play the game; by entering your domain. A hint all the way, a game I wish to play.

A trace that will have you living on the edge. Creating a warning, that will serve me well. It will hand me a key, a luck of the draw; just to intimidate me. Interrogating my mission, trying their luck by attacking vision holding on to my wisdom. A trace to track down those who complete the mission.

It was a turning point for me, I had no time to reveal another crime. Nor did I care where the corrupt were heading. As far as I was concerned, I was hoping without a word of lie they were heading towards a beheading. I was so over the edge, presenting the corrupt with a final pledge.

All I wanted, was to be left to be, feel safe and not let the corrupt get to me. They attached themselves to my spirit, feeding off my soul, returning for a rumour. Forcing me to recreate a challenge, where I hit the end of that trend. Then strive to compel, comprehend a tie; a dead end.

It was part of a past offence, a journey that caused the effects. It was the only way they could redo another clue hitting the corrupt right through. Where I was given, the all clear a chance to return and hit the corrupt in advance. Reversing that mission that handed me a proposition.

Given a challenge, led towards a vibe, handing me the passion to survive a dive. I was on the edge, of that ledge reviving a curse I could reverse recreating a turn of events. It was leading the corrupt towards a challenge that had me reliving another nightmare a threat that served me well in the end.

Warned of the chase that handed me a case. It was causing effects and returning for a trace. An opening had come to fruition and I was on the other end waiting for the invasion. Where I get a chance to deliver a feast to that measure that convinced me I had no reason to comply.

Nor follow up on another lie. Because the mission was based on a case that had served me un entrance to the unknown. I willingly was handed a key trapped in the middle of a case I could embrace. Handing me the incursion, I needed to rely on; only I to get by.

I was given a challenge a trace to embrace a case. It had me on the edge, a presentation that served the corrupt a trace I could erase. I was in a position I had to reveal, what I knew and who when where I was to review. Encourage the corrupt to redo, then follow up on another point of view.

In the end all I could sense was a trail of bad news, an error I could not rebel against. Because I was refused access, left to silently hit the end of that trend. Haunted by the past, reliving a present moment. I was following up on a key that fed off me; where each period ended in catastrophe.

It left me psyched up, following up on a conspiracy; hit me with a wondering eye. Causing effects and leaving me warned of what the corrupt were up too. I thought I was an intern to that imperishable; in fact, it was test for me to be replace it, hit an ending that was pending.

A beginning of a new trend, was forthcoming. Where I get in and track the corrupt down from within. A trace that was never to eventuate became state of the art. It was part of an investigation that had forced me to reveal another interrogation. A presentation revived an investigation.

What I had to do to prove my innocence, was not a journey I wanted to live. It was about to become worse than the lie. Because the rumours were unpredictable. It was part of a fight that handed me a fright. I on the edge of reason trying my luck to reveal revive a bad day. A dead end to that threat.

It created event, that that saved the corrupt and served them well, in the meantime. In the long run, I was runner up, ready to hit the corrupt. For if I had my way in then I probably would have hit them sooner with the same rumour. Leading them to a destination; forming another investigation.

I hit a dead end, it was causing an effect, it landed me a role to the next threat. Where the corrupt had a reservation, having me determine what end will hand me that trend. For I had to return and hit them with an interrogation, forcing them to abolish another investigation.

I had to go for a trip down memory lane, a journey that needed to repeat a game. Then redo that scheme that handed me the outcome, I needed redeem. For the forecast, was as followed, I was on the other end, forced to unravel a bend, to that trend. An investigation that will never end.

I was on the edge, aligned with the corrupt. Reading a passageway, with one hideaway. Holding on to a final getaway, a gateway towards a presentation. An initiation was to be repeated, where the trace was forced to replace a rude awakening. An image that lined me up for a clue; torn in two.

For the past, had opened up many unnecessary doors. It was part of a presentation, that made me see I was hitting the end of that catastrophe. An event that stated an investigation became part of that final. In fact, it took me on a journey to help me break the cycle that held me back.

An informative event, was caving in on the concept. They gave in giving me a chance, to hit the corrupt in advance. It was purely to help me focus on the truth, not the lie. Because it was the lie that got me out of the truth that was forcing me to hit the corrupt with a second trial.

It became quite farfetched how I was hit with a strong and effective debt to that trace that forced me to replace an entrance to the unknown it had me on the other end, getting back on track; spraying the corrupt with venom. Restoring my energy while deleting and delaying theirs.

Experienced as I was then, it taught me we; it had me locked in now. I was expecting a miracle, from the corrupts final. For they were intruding in my affairs, watching every move I made. Waiting for me to return hit back and finalise the impact. Where I get in hurry them up, and stepping forward.

Moving on, while I was waiting for the corrupt to return for a hit and run, was entertaining. It set me aside, set a light, saved me when I hit the right channel. Served me a dish, a side sample, a meal ticket on a silver platter. Faced me when I hit the end of that trend, then forced me to redo a clue.

Warned of the concept, an ideal momentum that failed me then was saving me now. I was given an idea that served me when I hit the end of that passageway. A stagnant foundation that had me pausing effects was Presenting them with a fear factor in the end of that threat.

It pushed them in the corner, had them locked in fastened from within. Waiting for me to return for another chance to pledge, in advance. For that reason, I was facing a made-up story in my head. Once and for all, ready for that drama to return look ahead; fast forward to get back on track.

No longer looking back, just stepping into the distance. It gave me a chance to replace that case. A moment for me to restore my energy. Meanwhile, in the mist of all evil I was saving my destiny. Hitting the corrupt with scrutiny, for that method of hitting me and running turned against them.

They saved me, trying their luck to harm me, for this time around I hit harmony. Where the corrupts unity had a challenge, it caused an effect and held me up. It led me on and created a foundation that forced me to return, hitting me when I hit the end of that informative event.

I was held up, without even having to enter their realm. It gave me a chance to return hit them in advance. Forced me to redo a trace I failed back when repeat it focus on a key, and rebuild a new foundation around the old the new and the energy that failed me right through.

It presented me with a valid point, a prejudice task that took me on a journey that prosecuted the corrupt. It handed me a faith that forced me to recreate a path to what I call a recall. A passage way to the end of that trend that had me cornered. Hit, ran forced me to regain consciousness again.

I was forced to reveal, a challenge that was surreal. I had to redo a never-ending battle just to feed off those who used me to succeed. It had served them a finally, and a hold up with denial in mind. For that was the only way

I could line the corrupt up for a first and last turn of events.

I was given outlook, to outrun that final challenge. So, when the time come, I was no longer in the loop, catching up, latching on, nor hitting the corrupt in the long run. It handed me a key and a trace that failed them tremendously. It took them on a path, that lasted a march, for they were stalling.

It had me on the edge, conditioning the mission and creating an opposition. It was landing me a role that served me whole. So, when I hit the end of that trend, the given moment will have me stepping into the unknown. Revealing what I assumed was part of the trend, forcing me to pretend.

I had no trace to overcast, for the feast was mine to release and finalise that piece. What I had was the beginning of an ending, that was pending. It forced me to retrace, those who encourage me to refine and feed of the ending. A challenge that was pending presented me with the divine.

A challenge II could erase all I had to do was repeat report and skip the corrupt too. All I had was end of that trend, that was hitting me. Hoping there was a case opened to discussion. It was part of the corrupts vision, that had me on the edge discussing what I thought was part of the last resort.

Those who returned to follow up on a key, forced me to repeat. An established outcome hit me long ago, forcing me to rebel against those who were harming me. For when I hit the end of the race. the challenge was charming me. It caved in on the alarm lining me up to hit scum with a hit and run.

For I was on the edge it had me alarmed, holding on to a case that served me well. It was presenting me with a forthcoming spell. Part of a road that lined me up for a final abode. So, when I hit the end of that vision, the interpretation will become part of the corrupts investigation.

Where I thought I was heading, had given me a chance to remain sane. It was part of a positive reflection, it had me on the edge presenting the corrupt with a key that served me well. For the pressure was on, it based on a past case. A given leisure to reclaim a division to the game.

What I assumed was part of a journey; interrupted me. A presentation to hand the corrupt a new trace, led me on, repeating a strong and valid shot, to polish up on a follow up. A mission that fed off me handed a declaration, a final reservation; when the time come, I could undo that clue too.

Moving forward was a part of a trace; it was handing me the conclusion I was longing for. It was throwing out the corrupts doubt, handing me the presentation to align me with a brand-new evaluation. So, when I reached my pinnacle, the journey I was on and once held brock the cycle.

I was handed a key that will bring forward unity. Annihilating the concept, causing havoc to every pause and effect. It was challenging me in a fight, leaving me stagnant without a bite. I was taught a lesson, a validation to that manifestation. left to silently, suffer while the rest remain humble.

I was put in a false position, led to believe the lie was part of my intuition. Where I played the game hit the end of that domain and had concluded. There was no resolution just the corrupt on the other end attempting to screw my head once again. Playing the game taught me a valuable lesson.

I was lied to, all along just to give the corrupt a chance to remain strong. For that made up story in my head was charming. It harmed me when I hit the end of that travesty. Helping the corrupt look ahead. Cursing every momentum claiming every truth so when I hit the end of that trend.

A retention of that trace, was replaced with a memory of a past case. An ending that was pending caved in on the concept. It was based on a key that left me revealing that everlasting contraption. A conspiracy that turned into a deception, forced me to undo and claim another vision.

I found myself protecting a vision that was forcing the corrupt to create a better opposition. It was causing effects leading me to a destination that had me on the other end reserving the right to disclaim another vision to a game that was gambling my journey away.

I was served well in the end of the race. A key that was interrogating me, had me forced to cause an effect. For I was on the other end, stepping into a dead end. Waiting for the corrupt to step in so I can step out and harm them from within. For the choices that were made were based on a cleanse.

It had me on the other end waiting for the corrupt to return and belt me again. They were feeding off the one thing that had me repeating a trace to that case. It warned me I was on the edge of rebelling against those who condition the mission; revealing a competition.

Repeating a new improved gamble to that view took its toll. For that rumour reached another level. For those who unveiled that trace took a gamble. It was part of a case that handed me a trace that served me well and presented me with an upcoming spell.

It was part of a given response, it had me on the edge revealing another pledge. It was creating an entrance to the unknown restoring my energy as I reach the end of that trend. It was feeding off the edge of reason. Presenting me with an expense, handing me the end of that conservative event.

It had formed me of an alliance, presenting me with a curse I could reverse. A trace that served me well when I hit that forthcoming spell. It handed me a presentation, that revealed the corrupts final interrogation. It forced me to return undo reveal one more truth. Before I hit the end of that review.

It was part of a personal vendetta, where I gave in paused an effect recreated a dramatic butterfly effect. It was purely to regain that gamble that hit me when

I hit the end of that trend. It presented me with a key. forcing the corrupt to rely on me to get in, assuming I was their meal ticket.

A trace they never earned to get in was a given. An energy to feed of that religious compound had starved the corrupt. A concept that presented me with a key caused an effect and praised me. For he who had it in for me hit, then ran stepping into a damn dead end; reaching the end of that trilogy.

Amen

CHAPTER 7

◆◆◆

WHILE THE CORRUPT WERE DIGGING I JUST PULLED THE PIN

A gas leak, has now erupted, I found myself in the middle of it. I fell into what I assumed was part of a conspiracy to embarrass me. For the corrupt were gas lighting me again. It was a trace that was trapping me in the middle of a praise. A warning they went too far trying to escape.

For they were trying there hardest to harm me frame and alarm me. They were so preoccupied into drilling fear towards my direction they did not consider the harmful effect of those who were in the middle of it. It was creating a force where the journey was to hit back with remorse.

It forced me to redo another event all while the corrupt were on the move trying to vent. The contest was part of the threat, it was to delve into a case that was feeding off the trace. It had me reliving another case. For I was in over my head giving out a vibe from within.

A minor dilemma, had come and gone. I was hit with a vengeance, warned of a key that was about to be stolen from me. This time around it served me well, not only it did not abandon me. It put me through a dry season, giving me a chance to hit the corrupt in advance; putting them through hell.

A chaotic effect, that had me on the edge, had restored my energy. It was warning me that the corrupt were planning to hit me run for the wrong reasons. Seasons had passed, I had to instil a challenge that force me to regain my conscious awareness again; waiting to be called up.

Only to witness the harsh truth. It was part of a plan, to harm me all by hurrying up. It was an ongoing, terror attack, a given energy to get back on track. A fighting chance for me to return speak my mind and follow up on a terrible lie. A trip down memory lane, that become part of the mission.

A tribe, that once knew me, and served me well then; has now turned against me. You think I would be surprised! Not at all; if anything, I was the one that created that drama. It was for I to return at a later date and rise above that fall. For those who served me well then; had no intention of repeating.

For that resurrection was part of a key, there were many who knew; wanting to screw me. Adding to my pain with scrutiny, causing effects and driving me insane. Assuming that will work, in fact my insanity has hit its peak; passing the humanitarian vibe a sense belonging no longer longing.

The game became part of a gamble and I was out to return for a scheme of my own. Just to hand the corrupt a dead end to that theme that served me well in between. It gave me a chance to redeem in advance scheming for a theme, while trying my luck to harm the corrupt and hand them bad luck.

I was returning for a repeat, a given moment to reach out. Then hit the corrupt with doubt, so when I hit my pinnacle the end result will no longer be pending and the trace will be never ending. I was forced to provide energy to those who assume they could stir the pot with a friendly shot.

They were on the edge, revealing a trace to embrace another case, it was causing effects and handing me a revelation to encourage me to release another mission to that competition. I was given the reason to return follow up on a key. To make matters worse they were hunting me down.

I gave in, purely to hand the corrupt a challenge to serve me from within. The edge of reason become part of my path that hit me when I hit the end of that trace that had me performing. I was afraid of what the outcome will be, for every challenge was to hand me a key.

The corrupt had other intentions, they locked me in kept me happy feeding off my wing. I was given a momentum a failed attempt to declare and disclaim that journey that was warning me again. For every time I sweetened the deal the end result will hand me salt to apply to the flame.

Where I had no intention of repairing another competition, just to remain solid again. Because I was given a cheap shot it forced me to relive a nightmare again. It gave me a chance to restore my energy in advance. Repeat a dream that was haunting me in between.

For what they were planning to do was harming me right through. It gave me the indication I was hitting a catastrophe not only I was fighting for my life. The end result was personally attacking me leading me to a destination that caused an effect and freed me from a curse I could reverse.

The journey I was handed was purely to keep me grounded. I was hit with an ending that was pending, and a trend that was never ending. I was always on the run trapping those who used me in the long run. It caused an effect forced me to resurrect and handed me a case I could erase.

I could not sit in one spot; damaged beyond repair. I was handed a challenge releasing a feast. It hit me right before I was handed an encore, a case I could erase. It conditioned my mission and reinforced a rivalry.

Stepping into the unknown had me assuming I was part of a group.

A challenge where in the end, I was left in the loop. If I played my cards right, I would come out the other end forced to pretend. Finalising that method that warned me. The key was final the only way out was hitting me with a troubled force. it had me forcing my way through failing right through.

It was hitting the corrupt, lashing out. They were laughing at me as I was there way out while I was handed out a key a line of bad luck. I was looking for a life line, a release I could not prevent because the challenge was harming those who assume. Hitting me and running will hand them a commune.

An event that will evaluate will have them convinced I was about to hit a dead end with a death threat. Where that confession will hand me redemption. For what I thought was part of a test. In fact, was part of a challenge that handed me the rope to hand the corrupt a chance to choke.

No longer shall I give in, hand them a free ride from within. For I was given an endowment to redo that forthcoming clue. It was part of a case to erase and follow up another feast. Where I released that piece and revealed what I was to do to repeat a challenge tracing the corrupts method.

A dream, that forced me to redeem a theme, had me conducting a séance in-between. Where I get in, advance my knowledge, and reveal the truth. Hunting the corrupt down, while I catch up and revive another dive. It had me releasing that demon to stay alive.

For the energy that prevented me from embracing the truth, caused an effect and handed me a key to resurrect. It also handed me a key to enforce the corrupt to reserve another serve. Purely to delve into the corrupts final hurdle, it was part of an industry to keep up with the program.

The energy that created the piece, restored my melody. It was a given, added with an indication I had reached my destination. Peaking, every time I was forced, to redo creating another avenue. Just to hand me revenue. It refined me, at every level, following up on what I thought was the truth.

The fact was, it became a constant reminder, I was carrying a heavy load of burdens. It left me returning to redeem a scheme, feeding off the corrupt in-between. It shoved a needle in-between the eyes of those who were challenging me in a fight. It traced trapped, handing me a level of delight

For the key that served me then, was nowhere near it was meant to be now. I had restored my energy by feeding off the curse, that took me on a verse, no longer fighting a lost cause. For the case became part of a trace, it took me on a measure I could treasure as I release pleasure.

All I had to do was conduct a clue, then release that feast that was hunting me down. So, when I hit the end of that lie, I was to be held hostage, no longer will I shine.

For they assumed it was a pointless for them to hand me kindness. Just Hand me any old key to keep me happy.

While the rest counteract and get back on track. Stepping into my realm as if they were welcome. In fact, the truth set me alight it forced me to rewrite my passageway. It was my heart that was holding me back, it set a precedent and pushed me off track; forcing me to decline.

For the energy that stated the fact also handed me the edge. Where I give in and then declare my innocence from within. Relying on no one but I to get by, causing an effect that had me lined up for a test I cannot regress. For the method that was handed to those who had a clue was pointless.

It had me on the edge, finalising that pledge. It was giving me an indication, I had no freedom nor foundation to rely on the corrupts final destination. I had concluded the fact; I was trapped in the middle of a confession. Where the corrupt were meant to return and hand me confusion.

I had no intention of returning to pretend. Nor even give them a chance to delve into a challenge in advance. For they were handed a key, a given chance to motivate me, just to cause an effect. Then when the time come create a foundation to unveil; the end of the Holy Grail.

A feast that warned me I was heading towards a beheading. It caused an effect and created a challenge that weighed me down. There was no breach to reach nor a trace to embrace, just a final case to encourage me to reach my potential and hit the corrupt at every avenue

Closing one door and opening another had me on the lookout. Looking further than the eye could see, warning me I had to follow up on a key that was harming. It was presenting the corrupt with a challenge like no other. They were trying their luck to hand me a chance, to withdraw and rebuild.

Because I hit a personal vendetta, the energy that served me caused a terror. I was stuck in the middle of a terrible lie, just to hand the corrupt a chance to get by. For that trace was part of a case that had me entering the unknown. It lined me up for a feast that had me step forward.

I was given an indication, I hit the end of a reservation. An invasion that had me on the edge protecting my soul from another threat. A beginning of a new case, that had me on the handed out an invitation to restore my energy. It forced me to release and feed off that feast.

It was the only way I could get back on track then finalise that impact. It had me stirring the pot, presenting me with a curse I could reverse. It was part of a key to serve me well and help me come first returning the favour so I can rehearse. A follow up on a hit that ended the case to early.

I was poisoned left to rise above and beyond. It created a door and a wall to make sure the corrupt enter no more. A catastrophe, where the corrupt stalked me and saw me coming. Where I decided to hit back with a forthcoming event. It lined me up for a dead end; forcing me to erase that case.

A trace to that method, had me on the edge. Trying to escape another dead end. It had me feeding off the energy that left me concerned. I was cornered pleasing he who broke my nerves. Stroking the head of he who wanted to get ahead. Assuming he can return, repeat, delete, delay, and get away.

It was a gamble, played back when; where the corrupt, got away with hitting me back then. I was led astray, left stagnant to my development. Wondering what I did wrong to be served such a reserve. I was held hostage left to suffer in silence. Given a challenge not worth its weight in gold.

I gave in, restored my energy from within, for I was given chance to regain my conscious awareness again. It lined me up for a winning streak, a rude awakening to get back on track. A need to condition the mission. Just to return and put the corrupt through hell; warning me I hit the end of that faith.

On the hope I return for a warmth; to my ideal dream. Where the energy, that had served its purpose then will give me the power to return now. Feeding off the key that faced an ending then presented me with a forthcoming event. It hit me, when the energy that failed me then; had died.

No lead, to restore nor a life line to divide a resurrection. For that journey was part of a trace, that hit me in the end of the race. It was causing effects, trapping me in the end of that dead end. Where that death trap that hit a holdup. A threat, handing me a conspiracy theory.

Hoping I would fail, and they have the last laugh. Assuming that will hand them the entrance to a starving mission. I was being forced against my will to reveal a competition. In fact, it was a trace that was part of a coverup. It lined me up for one more hit. A second trial to deny the corrupt vile.

I get in hit the corrupt from within, winning an inning. Stepping into a knowing was half the fun the other half was I getting in feeding off the corrupt from within. Creating a key to serve me well while I put the corrupt through hell. Causing an effect while making sure the corrupt never resurrect.

When I reached my pinnacle, the journey was to save me and serve me well. It gave me the trace I needed to get back on track. Feeding off the edge that was hitting me at the end of that trend. There will be no way of following up on a replay; for I gave in just before they were sent packing.

This time around, the corrupt, no longer had the power to outrun. Whether they outdo or even screw me right through; did not phase me a bit. If anything, I took the journey to high road followed up on a low line up of events. Lit up a candle and fed off those who fed off me; releasing a demon.

It took me on a journey that forced me to repeat. It restored my energy, while I fed off the synergy. I reached my peak hit a high note. Forced to release, hit back with the same feast. It took me on a journey that served me well, it freed me from that forthcoming spell.

Where I was on the move, forced to retrain my thoughts again. Just to find myself in the middle of a riddle. Conditioning the mission and failing the corrupt at every competition. Was returning to hand me revision. It had me facing my fear trapping those whom were dear to me.

Just to catch up feed off the corrupt; watching them give up. Because they were meddling in my affairs. A trivial event had trapped me giving me the indication I was to survive an added verification. It handed me the authenticity to replace that case that hit me in the end of the race.

It handed me the outcome I needed to key in, feed of the edge and present me with an upcoming event. It had me stirring the pot, on the edge retrieving a new lead. For that trace became part of a new lead. Just to encourage me to repeat replace and fail me in the end of the race.

It was part of a curse I had to rehearse, it had me restoring my energy so I can come first. But before I reversed back into that trace that forced me recreate a failed attempt. It gave me the lengthy period I needed to return and feed off the corrupt historically.

It was the only way I could restore the pages, revert to the end of all ages. Prepare myself to enter a trace that took effect, it hit me in the end of the race. It was presenting me with a key that took me on a journey. Serving me well as I rise above that poison that was imbedded into my blood stream.

A final triumph, had stepped into my realm, it gave me the energy that took me on a pathway towards heaven and hell. It had me step forward forcing me to release a feast. Warning me that the energy that served me well then case closed now. A chance I needed to release that feast.

A challenge I could revive, unless I fell into another damn lie. It was part of a realm that tore me to bits. It forced me to recreate a final count down. When the time come, I could review a clue. Encouraging me to revive a survival technique. Towards a skill that hit me; hinting the obvious.

Hitting the end of that trend, had me feeling ogre. I was oblivious to what was meant to come to fruition. Where I assumed I was hitting a challenge that was part of an upcoming clue. A curse I could reverse all I had to do was undo that impending review; a dead end to that trend

I was laughed at way too many times; it forced me to undo and finalise that review. Haunting me right through. It caved in on the concept, trapped the corrupt forcing it all to erupt. Trying my best to embrace a trace, Haunting the corrupt for they were constantly trying to get my attention.

Where at the end of the race, the trend was nowhere near it was meant to be. For the corrupt were to ruin my method by convincing me otherwise. They assumed they were it and they had the power uniting with a whole lot of misfits. I again had gone out of me way to solidify another bad day.

AMEN

CHAPTER 8

◆ ◆ ◆

FORCED TO CUT ALL TIES IGNORE THE POUNDING ON THE DOOR

I was on the edge, relying on the corrupts final test. I had returned for one more chance to release. Forced to condition the mission, then hand the corrupt a chance to hit me in advance. I had no choice I had to take a risk; it was to pay me out well, if I played my cards outright.

It had me escaping from a trace that was a dead end to me, at the end of the race. I had to finalise the entrance take a moment to review another sacrament. It forced me to release that feast that hit me well, when I was undoing that forthcoming spell.

I had one more cause of action, to incur, before I get in and feed off the corrupt from within. For I was on the edge of separating the old the new and the forthcoming clue. I was given a theme to redeem another scheme, then get paid out well troubling the corrupt as I go through hell.

It had me on the edge returning the favour, it fed off me while I was given the all clear. Trapped when I was heading for a feast, handed a clueless affair that served the corrupt unwillingly; having them fear the air. An obvious conclusion, for the corrupts method to backfire in the end.

Watching them step forward, had me step out, conditioning the mission then creating a challenge that forced me to repeat then hit the corrupt back about to undo a forthcoming clue. It was based on a trace that served me well at the end of that ritual. It forced me to redo a follow up on a clue.

It created a rivalry that served me well, it had me on the other end restoring a part of a case that had me pretending the key was never ending. Where I get in and have the corrupt surrender at every adventure. A challenge that had me preventing them from returning and attacking me again.

I was taken by surprise on a journey, farfetched from my reality. It had me facing an ending that forced me to reveal a past trend. It was harming me at every bend, reviving what I assumed was part of a game had ended up becoming a gamble all the way.

I had no idea I was hitting an entrance to the unknown. For I was entertained with the notion the corrupt were forced to reveal the end of that commotion. On the edge trying my luck to hit another trace, where the case served me well and presented me with upcoming spell.

It had me on the go, reviving another trace to that case. It served me well in the end of the race. Where I give in and case close that test that forced me to progress. It was handing me a key that led me towards a journey that had me on the edge gambling a trace to that feast; forcing me to release.

I was haunted in the end of the race, I had way too many rejections. I was handing out as much as I was given, it was the only way I could pretend I was heaving. Because the corrupt put the heavies on me it troubled me and I found myself hitting another entrance to my destiny.

I had no choice but to return and rejoice. Then hand the corrupt a failed attempt to hit me with a forthcoming event. The journey was no longer part of the outcome, the certainty was no more than extremity. The amount of energy I had to succumb to get through, was part of a follow up.

It gave me a chance, to fast forward to the next trace. A level of certainty, had come and gone, I was on the edge repeating another pledge. Where that challenge that led me to a listing. Was part of the corrupts method to lead me on, let me suffer on the hope I do not achieve another goal.

I was made out to be a fabricator, traced and trapped in the middle of a riddle. For an upcoming event that was poisoning me, had left me preaching my truth. It was presenting the corrupt with an ending that was pending. It forced me to repeat and follow up on a case that served me well.

I was on the edge, repeating a new trace. It was presenting the corrupt with a momentum, that served me well, at the end of the race. I was given a challenge, that was on the edge, of creating a new pledge. Where I was haunted by the past, living in the present.

Realizing firsthand, the corrupt were about to hit a dead end. There method of returning to harm me again, will depart and backfire. It will be part of a new development, where I get in and see my dream become a reality in between. Stirring the pot, undo a clue, create a reality I could live by.

It was part of a trace to redeem a scheme, then hit me back when. For the drama restored my energy in between. It was a dream to hand me the key to redeem a scheme forcing me to restore my energy as I get back on track. For I needed to reload and fast forward to the next final game.

A finally, where I win every test, periodically served well. I lit a flame, left it burning all the way. It presented with a key, that forced me to repeat an upcoming event. With no trace to replace, nor a cast to outdo. For there was no challenge less likely for me to retrieve; let go of or even strike.

I fell into a place, where the journey was to replace the old. Hold on to the new, with an ongoing review. It brought me relief, knowing what I knew was not true.

But I had to live that fantasy to create a better reality. Even though I knew the matter was totally indifferent; the game was real.

In the middle of a dead end, reliving the fantasy in the head; as if I was a teenager again. Making up unrealistic goals just to get back on track and repair an old wound. It was primarily part of a particle, a hint in the air, that was symmetrical. Embedded in my mind by he who knew.

I was led towards a destination of irrationality, substance abuse. God knows what else; if I gave in and believed it. For what tore me apart, was no lie it was a conspiracy to harm so I never get by. The hit was a gamble, the game was a scam and, in the end, I made it; reaching my summit.

I was exactly where I was meant to be. Holding on to one mental scar and that was? The Fantasy. The corrupts reality, where they assumed they killed me; with the wisdom of scrutiny. In fact, it saved me, it got me through, released a demon or two returning the favour.

It forced me towards an avenue handing me revenue. It drew me a line; a journey that served me well, during that forthcoming spell. For that dream now, has become part of my reality. A piece to that puzzle that was handed to me freely, it took me on journey that raised my awareness.

I had to follow up on a path, that had warned me in the past; I was not welcome. But the journey I was on made me energised by the concept and kept me strong. There was no way I was going to lose my way again. For I was forced to return drop another turn; an event, for my safety.

When I hit the end, an energy that forced me to pretend, had caused an effect. It handed me a chance to prove I was about to hit a dead end. Whether I was innocent or not gave me the incantation to repeat and hand the corrupt a final heave the one I needed to breath.

A replacement from the old, had me on the go. A stepping stone into the unknown, had come and gone. Personally, attacking the choices, I made. Making me assume those choices I made were wrong. In fact, it was part of a trace that served me well. Presenting me with an upcoming spell.

It kept me strong, occupied; preparing me for a new improved overzealous journey. A stepping stone into the unknown; solemnly on the go. Where I got in, stood back just to get a glimpse of another trace to that case that was about to harm me again. A past threat that hit me way below the belt.

I was left suffering at every level, heading straight into beheading. About to lose my light, forced to return hit back and feed off the edge. It was revealing another forthcoming pledge. The corrupt were about to hit me, then run finalising the outcome again. On another end, waiting for them to return.

A need to ease my pain, was broadening my horizons. A follow up on another safety net, served me well it gave me the challenge I needed to vent. Then when the time come overcome another outcome It had me surrendering the corrupts final bend. A given chance to hit back and pretend.

Where this time around I could not careless. For I resisted that possibility, that had me questioning every momentum. Leaving me forced to hit back, just to get back on track. I fed off that tact that hit me when I hit the end of that trend. Failing the corrupt while I reminisce again.

Another trace to that case that had me repeating final meeting, was paused. I on the other remembering the final to get back on track and feed off that poison that handed me denial. A given chance to laugh at that lie that was returning for a repeat.

Handing the corrupt a fight, where the task would be an impossible one to survive, in this life time. because I faced my fear fed off the trace that was dear to me. It gave me a chance to see I victimized commodity. All so I can catch up and finalise the ending that was pending.

Giving me the ending I needed to succeed, just to proceed. It was no longer part of that journey; I gave in and conditioned it from within. Presenting the corrupt with a final. An eruption leading them to a destination, where I reap a reward and hit them once and for all; with a first last recall.

Reserving the right to speak my mind, gave me a hint of strength. Where my sprit took over and hit back. I had to declare my innocence and decline whatever bad omen come my way. Where every time I hit the end of that trend the method that failed me then shall serve me well now.

I was handed a proposal, a need to feed off the corrupt. It was serving me well it gave me a challenge that had me face the corrupt head on. For they were attacking me inside and out it gave me a chance to feed off the trace and hand the corrupt a dead end in the end of that space.

An ongoing curse, handed me a challenge that cannot be reversed nor rehearsed. I was taken for a fool, given an opportunity to release peace then follow up on another key. It gave me the power and energy I needed to be free, for those who knew could not wait to screw me right through.

It was giving out vibes, stepping into a task I had to release just to find peace. Where I was constantly on the move, tracking down those who convey. All by conditioning the mission all the way. It had me consuming another union to that deception, forcing to reveal another redemption.

I was hit with a method that led me towards a destination, that gave me the power for confirmation. So, when I hit the end of that trend it forced me to pretend just to find peace in the end. it gave me the edge of reason facing me at every treason. All by attacking and bullying me just to warn me off.

Leaving me hunting for feasts, was caving in on me it was based on a trace that had me repeating another case it restored d my energy and had me on the edge returning for a new improved journey the one I needed to repeat reclaim and position the mission so I can remain sane in my domain.

There was so much animosity in the air, I could not step any further. The tension to that foundation was causing an effect and handing me the edge of reason so I can resurrect. I could sense a free ride to the other side with an outcome of murder. A fable to help the corrupt move further.

It was a made-up story in my head, just to help the corrupt get ahead. It forced me to heave at every scene; just to find peace. A failed attempt, where the corrupt had it for me, surviving another catastrophe. All because I fought back, instead of sitting back and remaining silent.

For they served me well and presented me with a forthcoming spell. So, when I reached that peak, it warned me of the outcome. A challenge that was serving me then, was restricting me now. I had a knowing that the corrupt were returning for hit run and a trace to overcome the outcome.

It had me holding on to ongoing event, it gave me the edge of reason, and a chance to vent. It forced me to reveal revive and hit the corrupt with the same game. A gamble to drain those who were driving me insane. An ongoing event that served me well, forced me to rethink that spell.

Even though their plan was prewritten, I knew in my heart the corrupt had a prewarning. Prewriting my script was not part of my mission. If anything, I was back on track repeating a condition. For the mission was prewritten. An energy to endeavour and devour to the next proposal.

My walls collapsed; I was given a chance to hit back. Where I decided to relapse, release a feast, raise the buck, and then give up. Just to give me a chance to repeat another cover up. It was handing me a key, conditioning mission so I can preach my truth; entering the competition with repetition.

Without any limitation, I was given a proposition, to release my inhibitions. It was part of a composition that had me hitting right in admission. A mission that became part of a trace was just my assumption. The truth was they saw opportunity to hit run, then reveal another outcome.

It had me on the edge creating a pledge, where the corrupt were handed a key. It led me to believe that the trace was a case; failing me at the end of the race. It had me attempting to embrace that one thing I needed to get in. handing them bad luck. A given chance to release find peace.

It was part of a vision, I on the edge, pretending I knew nothing. Just so they can continue to feed off me, preventing me from reliving my destiny. It was leaving me hunting for a fight. A feast to hand the corrupt a chance to release. Warned beyond recognition; about to repeat a hint of madness.

For the journey I was handed left me branded. For

I had a technical issue, an expense that was forced by those whom were contempt. It led me towards a journey that forced me to undo a forthcoming clue. I was given a presentation that hit me at the end of that investigation.

It gave me the energy to release and follow up on another lease. It meant I had nothing to do with what drama was heading my way, at the time. All I knew I was given a new identity. It had me on the edge, laughed at that path I was handed, for in the end I had to rejoice entering a new phase.

I needed to repeat, replace put the corrupt through hell and evert. Presenting them with a forthcoming spell. A given freedom to repeat that meeting. It forced me to reclaim a division dividing the corrupts method into three sections. Firstly, with no questions asked; Undo the clue.

Secondly screw he who knew. Watching him scream for mercy in between. Thirdly without a lie only speak the truth. A given chance to report those who knew, pushing them in the corner; skipping that too. Time to repeat, hit back the same. Making sure the corrupt were afraid to retaliate.

Returning for a hit will gamble the corrupts method. For I was given a chance to reveal that scheme. It was purely to force that remorse out so I can catch up and hand the corrupt doubt. It caused an effect hit back and fed off that debt. It had me ready willing and able to reveal another fable.

It had me poisoning the one thing that was keeping me real; from within. It failed the corrupts the fake and false accusations. For energy I was handed created an empire, that ended in tragedy. The method collapsed, picking up the pieces that was left behind. Making me out to be a fabricator.

Assuming I was to blame for breaking the cycle. Had the corrupt were to return for a yearning. It gave me a chance to repeat, proving I was innocent, pressing delete. It had me questioning every motivation stepping into a case that held me to contempt; giving the corrupt no entertainment.

For those who stood their ground had me on the edge, revealing another gamble. An ending that repeated, where the drama took over and I was given a fight. A chance to hit back and suffocate the corrupts method so I can get back on track. It caused an effect and had me restoring my energy.

I was hit with an ending, returning with a scheme; trapped in between. It had daunted on me how strong the corrupt had gone. Where a string of events messed up my head, it was handing me the conclusion. Where the only case that was to be erased was the one that hit me in the long run.

They were obsessed with me, trying their luck to hit me then run with bad luck. It had me on the other end warned of what I call the end of that recurring attempt. A detailed event purely to prevent the corrupt to return for a recall. A thread that had dropped into a dead end.

It was revealing the corrupts final deal, in the end. It served me well just so I can look ahead feeding of the trace that forced me to replace a forthcoming event. It gave me a chance to get up get back on track. Then hit the corrupt at the end of that threat.

AMEN

CHAPTER 9

◆ ◆ ◆

HAPPY DAYS AHEAD BECAUSE THE CORRUPT HIT A DEAD END

There was a moment in the air, where I was given an opportunity to scare the hell out of the corrupt. It caused an effect and hammered them in the head. Long enough for me to get ahead, assuming they had the power to hit back. A given chance to starve the corrupt by handing them anguish.

In the end, I could not pretend, any longer. For those who knew had me on the edge revealing another clue. For the trace was a case that served me well. It left me wondering what the hell did I do to deserve such a serve. Handed me a key, restoring my energy then feed off the concept.

A challenge that will set me up for life and free of anomaly. I was presented with a task, that had me on the edge. A final cover up, that handed me a clue and a chance to feed off the edge of reason. It was presenting the corrupt with a challenge they could undo.

Forcing me to repeat, had me switched on. It gave me the entrance to the unknown. Expressing my gratitude was hinting the worst it gave me the indication I hit a burst of energy. It had me forced to reclaim and divide that mission handing me the competition to revive another vision.

The journey I was on had me conditioning the evaluation to that manifestation. It was part of a mission that was giving me a chance to return, hitting the corrupt in advance. Where I get in and repeat that competition, from within. It was presenting the corrupt with one more mission.

It gave me a chance to return, warning them that I was on the move. Relying on no one to catch up Because I caught up and hit the corrupt with a dead end in the end. It had me on the move reaping a reward that took that challenge to another level. Giving me a chance to end that task in advance.

The follow up was part of a cause, it was a case I could return and hit back with remorse. A trace that will resemble what I thought was part of an uncanny remark. It had me on the second trial second best, hitting the corrupt with denial. It was part of a trend that forced me to return and clear the air.

A trend that was repeating, gave me a chance to hit back then follow up on another meeting. It served me well then hit me with a final a constant reminder the thirst was overcast the last draw was under taken it gave me the reason to repeat and reply for another treason.

It had given me a chance to restore my energy in advance. Returning for one more chance to return in and feed off the corrupts delusion handing me restitution. For what I thought was an ending that had me surrendering at every meeting, was a pass. Purely to catch up; feeding off the corrupt.

An ending that made me see that the tragedy that was pending; a never-ending catastrophe. Evidently so I can prove my innocence again. What a waste of time and energy where this time around I was returning for a feast a cast to wrap it up for one more chance to repeat.

It was to press delete delay presenting the corrupt with an outcome all the way. Just to hand me the key terrorise them, then hand them a new improved guess. A trace they can replace, all so I can harm those who harmed, assuming they got the power to condition the mission.

It was creating a proposition, a challenge that had me undo and encourage the corrupt to return and repeat another game. It was gambling my journey and driving the corrupt insane. For the gamble became a terrible lie, it served me well and handed me a forthcoming spell.

I needed to put the corrupt through hell. The only way to do so was create a challenge that forced the corrupt to return and follow up on a feast that had me hitting another lease. It repeated reported and trapped the corrupt in the middle of an upcoming riddle.

It forced me to indulge into the unknown then when the time come repeat report and rebel against that upcoming spell. it had me repeating an everlasting condition. it forced me to repeat and hand the corrupt the end of that trend that led me towards a journey that warned me.

I was about to be hit with an expense that repeated and handed me a delay. It was the only way they could return and press replay. No longer delaying the inevitable. Because the journey I was on sold me out and left me suffering so the weak can remain strong.

What an omen I had to revive just to state a fact and stay alive. A waste of a case, that was challenging me in the end was handing me the purpose I need to pretend. It gave me the urge to submerge into the unknown then when the time come clear the air and claim a gamble to the game.

An outcome that served me well in the long run. It had me forced to cause an effect repeat a trace. It was embracing a case condition the mission to get back on track, following up on a competition. It was ending with a trace that was challenging me in the end of the race.

A pending situation that repeated, handed me the upper hand to restore my energy. It was purely to press delete, no longer delay because I was in demand. I have no time than the present to create an atmosphere, I could hardly see. Because the corrupt had conspired to harm me.

It was interesting how they could have me on the go, creating a challenge that served me well. It was the only way I could get in undo that clue and create a way in. Where the corrupt had me hitting the finals. A review that served me well and gave me the energy I needed to go through hell.

Where I was on the go spraying venom creating a trend. Then when the time come feed off the energy that served me well in the end. It was a given and I was handed a key a challenge to hit the corrupt with a catastrophe. For the entrance to the forbidden was no longer prewritten.

I was given a chance to return in advance. It was to follow up on a condition, that forced me to redo and create an outcome I can screw up and present the corrupt with a case that cannot. It was repeating what I thought was part of a case, it had me revealing a revivification to that destination.

For I had one more chance to trap and trace the corrupt in advance. It forced me to repeat undo and reclaim a faith to that method that restored what I thought was part of an encore. It repeated handing me a clue. It was forcing me to undo one more point of view.

A faith less likely for me to repeat then return for one more key, had me stepping into the unknown warning the corrupt they were forced to reclaim a division to the game. A dead end in the end gave me a challenge that served me a clue. They saw me coming and handed me a forthcoming spell.

It trapped he who knew and presented me with one more clue. Just so I can finalise that review. A follow up on another wrong move. A point of view. That had me hunting down those who returned and repeated another trace to that case that had me stepping into the unknown.

Reclaiming another gamble to that scheme that hit me in-between. It forced me to restore what I thought was another part of a key that had me returning just to cave in on the concept and press delete. So, when I reached my peak, the ending would become part of a trip down a memory lane.

A treasure to that trace, forced me embrace that one upcoming dilemma. It lined me up for one more clue, a presentation that served the corrupt well and hit me with one more review. It was ongoing and the only thought that gave me a clue handed me the entertainment so I can redo.

It was part of follow up, where the key handed me the energy to recreate a final synergy. The one that served me well and put me through what I thought was interesting because the corrupt were hinting the worst that had me on the other end returning for one more trend.

Where I was on my own, stepping forward, while I catch up. Hitting the corrupt with one more go. Giving me the entertainment to repeat report and follow up on a case that presented me with one more trace. a feast that will hand me release, trapping those who attempted to trap me.

Where in the end of that trend, the only thing that had me returning for a win. It caused an effect and created a deception just to repeat report and follow up on another redemption. It forced me to case close that trace hit the end of the race and personalise the tread so I can catch up.

It had me repeating a trend to that method. It had me on the other end trying my luck to cancel out another sense of bad luck. Where I was given the all-clear sense that the end was part of a trend it forced me to redo catch up and finalise another forthcoming clue.

I was given a chance to hit back in advance. Stepping into the unknown ready and willing to reclaim another God Willing. Where I was on my own warning the corrupt, I hit the end of that trend. It was causing effects and harming me again. For what I had to do just to find peace was alarming.

It was revealing what I thought was part of a key. It forced me to repeat and condition the mission applying for one more competition. A forthcoming event to drop in, one more thump, handing me the key I needed to repeat reclaim and fast forward to the next final claim.

Just before the corrupt were to repeat another coverup. I had a warning; it gave me the incantation, I was on the edge repeating a gratification, to the next final destination. Refining a confirmation. Where I was a victim of scrutiny again the only way out; was hand me, a key to get out.

It was purely for them to skip me too; it was warning me there was no entrance to the unknown. Just a challenge to hit the corrupt when I hit the end of that trend. It was giving me the energy to repeat report and create an ending that had me haunted by the past.

The made-up story in my head, was meant to last a life time. In fact, it created an entrance that forced me to redo, cause an effect, repeat a defence to my method. It was skip that too, hitting an ending that was pending. Considering the fact that I was given a chance to get back on track.

I was hitting an entrance to chaotic event. It was leaving me trapped warned of what tomorrow will bring. It had me warned of what the drama of what the drama will bring in the long run. leaving me running for my life. Assuming the corrupt knew and could not wait to finalise; one more clue.

It forced me to redo a follow up, on what I thought will give me a trace, to hand me an informal case. It had me on the edge, presenting the corrupt with an invasion. A constant reminder I hit the end of a debate rewarding me where I was on my own hitting an ending that was pending.

For that key, that was forced to recreate a trace, made me see I hit another internal investigation. It had me stepping into a method that hit me right at the end of that trace. It warned me I was on the edge, presenting the corrupt with a curse I could reverse. All I had to do was come first.

It had me presenting, the corrupt with a foundation, reliving an informal investigation. I was given a trace to release that demon that handed me the energy to hit back. Presenting me with a key all while I get back on track it alarmed the corrupt. A willing to undo and follow up on another clue.

I was handed an outcome, where I need to replace a case. It had me entertained, thinking of ways to remain in the game. Stay in the moment, as if I was watching a screenplay, in fact it was part of a real-life scenario where the journey had me reliving a nightmare; but in someone else's eyes.

My thoughts went wild, because my presentation had hit me with denial. Because the curse had reversed, the right to accommodate another fight cased closed everything. It was enough for me to witness I hit the end of that tether and decided to return for a vendetta.

The trace became a gamble, it left me repeating another scheme. For I was on the edge of reason reviving another treason. I had trapped the corrupt in the corner, warning them that this time around I am over the threats. The trace the treads I am even over the corrupts final debts.

Not only, I was not interested in what the corrupt had to offer. The game was a gamble, it was a waste there was no time than the present to undo a clue. It was purely to return for one more chance to advance and hand the corrupt a challenge where the only way out will be six feet under.

For my knowledge to hit the corrupt with a chance to undo. Was part of a follow up, that had me on the with a new tread breaking the cycle. I was hit with an allegation that made no sense to my destination. Part of a clue that hit me when I hit the end of that review.

I was to take that challenge to another level, then advance my knowledge. For the journey was part of a task that had me on the edge repeating and reclaiming another force to that cause. It lined me up for one chance to hit back with remorse. It was part of a trace that had me on the edge.

Presenting the corrupt with new improved journey. Handed me a chance to step into the unknown. It was creating a presentation that lined me up for another investigation. I was given a chance to hit back in advance, a challenge that was instigating a fight had me investigating the reason.

It would have harmed me if I hit back to early, for the journey was serving me wrong. It was giving me the indication I hit the end of that trend that was warning the trace was part of a dead end. It was case that conditioned the mission and reclaimed another competition.

I had no chance in hell of repeating another meeting. Because the journey I was on had me challenging the wrong. It gave me the chance to protect what I thought was part of that contest. I was given a manifestation to repeat and hit the corrupt with a final investigation.

An indication I was hitting the corrupt with a final investigation brought me forward. Alarming me no longer, because the journey was ready to ponder. For it was causing an effect and harming the corrupt at every resurrection. That is when I knew I hit the end of that deception.

I was given the structure that I needed to restore my energy and feed of the corrupt. A faith less likely to succeed the right presentation that will come my way. It will give me the challenge I need to succeed and the power to unveil another bad day. Revealing the corrupts presentation all the way

The task was to undo the one thing that served me well from within. It was presenting me with an upcoming event, that had me causing effects and debating what end I should take and what journey will give me the power to partake and follow up on another trace.

It was uncanny how many times I was given a chance to return and follow up on a clue. It served me well and presented me with an upcoming spell. Handed a challenge with an outcome that forced me off the edge. It led me towards an encounter that had me threatened; living on the edge.

I was taken on a pathway, referred to another dead end. Serving me a sentence that gave me the power to return for a vengeance. For the outcome that took me on, and led me towards a dead-end, A journey that served me well in the long run. It repeated handing me a case I can erase.

A challenge I cannot face, had me on the edge protecting the corrupt, long enough. Just to have them, and keep them guessing wrong. Hand them a fake accomplishment, then follow up on a key that will serve the corrupt a trace that will close the case. Repeating another forthcoming meeting.

A force to redo and follow up on another clue. It had me recreating a final review. All I had to was come forth, hit the corrupt right through. Handing them the key I need to return and spray venom at those who sprayed in my direction. Forcing them out the door alarming the corrupt once more.

They will hit the end of their destiny forcing me to repeat. Where this time around I create a piece that will wake up the dead. Just to come and save me from the living dead. To bring forth harmony to my destiny, a journey that will bring Peace to humanity killing the Demon who stands in my way.

HALLELUJAH

CHAPTER 10

◆ ◆ ◆

WHAT IS STOPPING YOU CORRUPT!

Feeding off the presentation that fed me from within. Handed me a curse to reverse while I delete delay and harm those who think harming my spirit will hand them reason to live. Where I get to see the future and transcribe while I scribe, the manuscript; that will bring the end to Humanity.

I had stepped into a mind reading game, I could sense the reality take over my train of thought. There were several in the picture trying their luck to hit me with bad luck. Just so they can get a glimpse of a future event and leave me trying to fix another threat.

I gave in back then I was way ahead of them that game

they trace me with was a gamble it had me on the other end trapped in the middle of a dead end. Troubling those who knew and could not wait to enter my realm and hit me with an extra kick a final reveal before I entered the club once more.

It was now or never and the trace was a given a challenge that was over ridden. It gave me a clue it forced me to redo and develop another point of view. A thing of the past was beginning to last not only I was returning for a vendetta. But the journey I had been handed was haunted me.

It landed me in a role that had me stranded. It had me questioning the motives of those who were involved; it caused an effect and hit me with another dialect. Where the method was prewritten and the journey that I was handed left me branded. It was so well done by those who knew;

It had me turned, where I realized right through that the prediction was part of my resurrection. It gave me the power to reserve the right to return hit back and devour. For those who divided and concurred had been stabbed back. I on the other end transferring a challenge trapping them again.

The journey was for me purely to get me back on track; it was a given. Not a motivation to recreate another conspiracy. Because every journey had me warned that the corrupt were on my raider. Waiting for me to break that cycle they can depart deport and restart.

It gave the corrupt a chance to repeat another hit. So,

when I got in, I could return at a later date and finalise the entertainment, to bring love and hand me hate. All by handing them a dead end to that train of thought. It had them returning to repeat and stalk me again.

But this time around I was ready for that hunt down. Not only I made it to the finish line, but the debt became a threat. It handed me the knowledge I needed to hit the corrupt back and return for a line up. Where the trace became part of a case that took me on journey and repeated a scheme.

I was given a reason hit the corrupt with a death threat. Leaving them hunting for a feast where every time I was given a challenge the end result will land them a role to undo and create a forthcoming event. Handing me the key to get back on track and screw those who screwed me.

It had come to my attention, the corrupt were hitting me with redemption. Then every so often they would take the initiative return for a pick me up, assuming that the journey was part of a clue. In fact, it was a trace that had me on the edge repeating a new pledge.

I was handed an interference, left to suffer in silence. All while the corrupt return to terrorise me again. But this time around, I had made my mark and that free ride that served me then was the way in it gave me the power to suffocate the corrupt from within.

It created the piece to follow up on a new lease. Desiring every method just to find peace. Where my suspicions were clarified and the corrupt were planning another hit. Where this time around I enter there stir the pot hint how to hit back and watch them as I block them surrender and combust.

As they rot, I continue on my journey hitting the corrupt with every yearning. For I took over the energy that created a second trial. The one that was leading me to denial, handing me the truce. Hitting the corrupt right in the middle of a challenge where the riddle became a spindle effect.

It was a given; a challenge with no momentum to spare. Just a predominant energy that was printed with prominent air. It was dominating the whole concept, trying its luck, to return and hit me with bad luck. That when I knew, the energy that was part of the corrupts synergy, caused an effect.

The journey I chose eased my pain; I went through a thorough investigation. Just to come to terms with the fact the corrupt were on my raider stepping into a challenge that had me undoing another feast to that piece that was forcing me to release peace.

I was warned, that there was no certainty, to that method. It had me working under cover, I was always on the run, creating an energy to hit whom; in the long run. Just a cover up that mess that was haunting me in the past for I assumed it was mistake; in fact, it was part of my journey.

A challenge I cannot repeat delete delay nor even accommodate another journey along the way. It had me reserved for a foundation to line me up for an investigation. It was repeating another meeting; hit me with an investigation to warn me the nest trace was part of a key.

An inquisition to that final recognition, caved in on me. It had me restoring my energy and returning for another yearning. It handed me a chance to hit the corrupt in advance. Freely sacrificing those who caved in on the mission; handing me another competition.

A chance to repeat a second trial; caused an effect. It had me stepping into the unknown. Denied access; all while the corrupt kept feeding off me. Where I was in the mood of giving in and handing out another clue. Handing out more than I could handle; because I was hit with a scandal.

Handing out just as many death threats as I was given. Gave me the first and last chance to hit the corrupt in advance. A forbidden injustice, was being formed behind my back. A give chance to get back on track. Handed a final review and a new improved restitution to that evolution.

Where I had my days numbered and the task at hand serving me a clue. It was creating a better avenue, and serving me well at every final review. An entrance that I needed to repeat had me on the other end returning to press delete. A favourable momentum serving me well at every section.

Where a final giveaway came before me. I was given a challenge that warned me. before I enter the unknown, I could embrace another case. It had me handing the corrupt a step into a path way of creating a curse I could reverse. A journey that will serve me serenity in the long term.

That eternal bliss, was an essential element to me. It had me questioning the motives, of those who had the idea that I was weak. Because I lacked the unity, in my vicinity they assumed, that entrance was prohibited. Hitting and tormenting me in my domain left me strained suffering in silence again.

Little did they know, I was building a foundation, around the journey that was offered. I had no choice I had to play Judas just to rejoice. For the one thing that failed me then, hit me from the ground up. I hit the end of that trace and was served a key just to find solitude from within.

For the corrupts final degree, warned me I was nowhere near, where I was meant to be. An absolute disgrace had come and gone. It Made me out to be part of a scheme, it was forcing the corrupt to return for a rude awakening. Where they saw me easy terrorising me with a conspiracy.

I had way too much work to do, I had no time to mix; with those who wanted to fight me. The energy that had, me surviving on that air had created a flare. It gave me the opportunity to return for unity handing me the conclusion I needed to hit the corrupt with delusion and confusion.

Cleaning up the mess, as I watch the corrupt give in and confess. Had me forming an alliance of my own accord.

I was given an opportunity to use those who were used to harm me. Following up on a reminder there was a con-artist in the mist. Hitting the edge; presenting me with a cover up.

A reliability that become defiant to my creativity caused an effect. It had me searching for answers, just to find peace. Because the corrupt were on my raider raiding my head. It took me a life time to come to terms and the realization I was being stalked by he who knew hiring he who had a clue.

A damnation, that caused an effect and took me on a journey that was harming my spirit. It had me warned and wondering where I was heading how the conclusion hit me with a beheading. So, when I hit the next conviction, the vision will leave me endowed while the corrupt remained impaired.

Blind sighted by the trace that had me reliving another case. It had me restricted forcing its way through. It relisted a trace that was casing me at the end of the race. Casing every final challenge that come my way it was feeding off the one thing that handed me the power from within.

It harmed my existence, lined me up for a competition. Where I saw light, with extraordinary vision because I had premonition. Completed my task met my quota mastered my craft. Warning everyone against me, was serving me a resilience. Allowing me to return and terrorising their inner Demon.

Where I stood my ground, stepping into a catastrophic

event. Hitting the corrupt with the notion they had me at piety. A definitive effect, where the only game that served me well. Was the one that led me on, and put me through hell. Hitting me with the fact I was on my path.

Where leading the blind, will hand me an antagonistic point of view. A thought wave I needed to come to terms with the fact the corrupt were about to hit a dead end. A trend that was forcing me to return and pretend. Feed off their fresh start and lead them towards starvation.

No reservation, nor a chance in hell, to hit me with deviation. For a repeat, to that gamble was inevitable. I was on the go, had lots to do, and no time than the present to complete the task. A service well done, when I hit the end of that methodology. A review, that had me leading the pact.

I was on the cusp, of trapping those who knew. An indication I was stepping into another complication. Burnt by the past trend, then returning with a resurrection from that redemption again. Was part of another game one that had me gambling my dream away.

Where I was given a chance, to short list the corrupts game in advance. Just to enter the unknown, with a repeat, then try to my luck to hit back with a karmic effect. Just to get a hint of what to expect. It gave me a second chance to hit back in advance. What it was worth the curse come first.

It was based on that upcoming event; it left me struggling to come to terms with the facts. For the corrupt were way to ahead of me waiting for me to fail. All so they can return steal another key, because in the past I was so cut open the anxiety took over and the corrupts final trap.

It had me following up on a key that took me on a journey that was suffering me. There were walls collapsing, challenges relapsing and whole lot of dreams that failed me along the way. In the end I gave in, handed the corrupt a dead end to that trend; It had me harming my spirit in the end.

I went through it all, reached my pinnacle, following a path that was cynical. It had me on the move, hitting the corrupt at every groove. A pleasure that had added to my charm, had me stepping into another trace to that case. It forced me to repeat a hit of a hint at the heat of the moment.

A warning every finally had a false reading. No truth in the outcome. Stepping into the unknown just to pass a test, hit the corrupt with a final conquest. For what I assumed caused the effects, was part of a conclusion. It was to hit the corrupt with a final request; a trace I could replace.

It was part of a resolution, that had me questioning the motives, of those who saw me easy. For the one key I earned and managed to use periodically; had come and gone. Where the key was nowhere near the corrupts final entity. I was Involved in a world parting ways from a lifestyle; lived and let go.

What was meant to happen, did not come to fruition,

the way it was expected. For there was a shift in the universe, I was to fight back a line-up of freedom that had me scheming for more. I had to get back on track lift my spirits with a burden on my back. Then go back and rectify that terrible lie.

A rumour that forced me off the edge, had taken its toll. For I hit a high note, added with a hold-up. A curse that served me well after I went through hell. I was torn in two directions, neither of them worked well for me. Left to suffer, venture on my own for the corrupt did not do me the favour.

Pushed in the corner, and tracked down by those who were harming me behind the scenes. Had me alarmed, because what they were planning was a joke. It was part of a conspiracy to hit me and run with a certainty in mind. They were on my raider, waiting for the right moment to face me.

Then hit run, just to see me fail in the long-run; kindly tell me why? It had me turned, assuming they could get away with it; troubling me. The decision to play it, and trick them too, let go finalise the review. When I hit the end of that calamity the method, will change; handing me the key.

A need to reserve the right to succeed, was a task I could not let go of. I was given a challenge ready to reap another reward. An evolution to my resurrection, just to change the way I saw society. For the scene became obscene. Obsolete, trying my luck delay put the corrupt through hell all the way.

When the curse was reversed it turned into a travesty. It served me well handing me the key to the next final review. For it was the individual belief, that turned me around. It made me sense there was no justification to that journey because the corrupt were serving me wrong.

It was handing me the trend to remain strong. Create an alliance of my own a piece that will follow me up onto the next beat of the drum. Wanting so desperately to create a worldwide catastrophe; just to find peace was forming self-pity. Towards those whom were somewhat wittier than I.

They served me wrong; stringing me along. It was way too early to come out and follow up on another clue. For I was given a challenge to set a precedent. Trying my luck to get over the bad Luck. That took me on a journey fighting off those demons; that were harming me.

When I hit that travesty, I was given the all clear to return and create a trace. It served me well at the end of the race. Having said that the method in itself was a motivation that served me well at every germination. It held the corrupt up caused an effect and handed them bad luck.

For that omen was way too harsh to follow up on. Where that scheme had me on the edge creating a new theme. For I was given an opportunity to reclaim my difference. Forced to reveal a conviction to my mission. Just to find my way through and hand the corrupt a feast; they cannot piece together.

It was part of a trust creating a trough. Purely to justify the action, of why my demons took over the mission. Tricked me into an oblivion, believing that the lie was only to come true if I followed the right path. It was sacrificing the one thing that kept me from living that dream from within.

I had a high moral standard and my beliefs were outdated. The corrupt assumed my ancient views were unbelievable. Nevertheless, it was my innocence that served me well during the conquest. The facts were obvious, the claim became part of my domain; where each journey was God willing.

It was to make sure what ever happened next, I would have the power to repeat another test. The energy to make sure the corrupt confess; handing me the evolution. I need to resolve the case then forced, to redo a final review. Lining me up for deception; not part of that redemption.

For the corrupts way of leading me towards their direction was part of a vendetta. Where in the end I found that method and threat quite amusing. I had no time to spare nor did I wish to sit around and compare. The competition was way too easy to compete and compel; because that trace was fake.

For that individual they hired to compete had no strength over me. It was based on the power of he who knew and he who had a clue. Mine was based on experience alone my lifestyle that was chosen for me was based on a future creativity and the urge to skip escape and create an aloof.

An attempt to sweeten the deal, had formed a curse I had to reverse. For I came first, a follow up, had presented me a faith less likely for me to fail. The corrupt knew where I was heading, they created the piece by hunting me down. A piece, I had to release informing I had no peace.

They found opportunity to take over my journey. Manipulating the situation at harmed me at every resurrection faced with a key at every contrast. For he who knew had a contract written without my consent. A Manipulation, added with an addiction, to attain a resolution to their restitution.

A concept I never agreed to, for those terms and conditions were a lie. It was based on a feast to hand me the case that served me well. It presented with a forthcoming spell. For that past event changed I fell into heap at the heat of the moment. Disguising the corrupt at every motivation.

The contracts were void not breached. For the conditions were based on a case that forced me to erase that condition. It had me on the edge presenting the corrupt with new improved trend. A hint to the obvious had me on the second trial. No longer shall they have that laugh, in the end.

My exit to that journey was forcing me again to lay low. It gave me the energy I needed to feel safe. The corrupts attempt to forge my signature was a dead-end. Where the walls collapsed, and the journey was up to date.

Creating a presentation, to hand me a relapse to the next destination.

Assuming they could hit me run had forced the game to come to a hold up. It was creating an extended warranty from within. An outcome that hit me in the long run, that managed to return, repeat, and follow up on a key from within. A journey that had me forced to recreate a second trial.

The way it was stated, was meant to be created with peace in mind. A journey that had me in knots. belted me from within. It took me on a passageway that trapped me, serving me unwillingly. All so I fail and never win. Leaving me dropping that bombshell from within, while going through hell.

The partial reason I hit the end of that treason was because the corrupt saw me coming. They wanted to hit me and run me down with a forthcoming event. Just so they can return take another crack on getting on my nerves. Assuming that will regain their conscious awareness again.

Where the outcome warned me of the truth. It faced me with a key that had me repeating a curse I could reverse. What a last laugh I was carrying on my end, for the burden was a claim to clean up the mess and have the corrupt confess. It was to hit me when I hit the end of my domain.

It gave me the energy to hand me a clue. It released that demon that had me suffering in silence right through. For I needed to come first at last and release that demon.

Forcing me to wrap it all up independently. It handed me that case that was warning me I hit the end of the race.

I was free from anomaly, safe from a journey, where the corrupt took me in and used me as bait. It served me well and gave me the forthcoming spell. It saved me initially and initiated a line up to the next task. Meanwhile I took the initiative trapped within, get in finalising the next ideology.

A challenge that hindered the next of kin, served me well. It handed me a chance; to delve into a journey, forcing me to advance and accomplish a goal. It presented the corrupt with an upcoming spell. For they assumed that they could enter my realm, entertaining me with a false notion.

An accusation that reinforced me to repeat, trapped me in the middle of that upkeep. It reclaimed a challenge that took me on a path way, towards the corrupts direction. A journey that will haunt me if I did not face my fear. It was a given, a well-presented outcome; to put the corrupt through hell.

For what I had to do, just to end the game sooner served me a clue. It gave me a chance to repeat and remain silent in the end of the game. Whenever they saw me fit the thought they could return and hit me again will, become a failed attempt on their end.

Because the corrupt were torn in so many directions, trying to get my attention. Attentive as I was, I gave in on the condition I feed off every inning. Handing them a dead end to that outcome, for the energy that served me well. Handed me the key, that forced me off the rails.

Straight into a second trial. For I was taught well by those who knew me well. For the journey was clinging towards the wrong path. It handed me the cause and effect to pause. Whatever warned me I was hinting at the end of that threat. It forced me through warning me there was no up keep.

Just a challenge to remind me where I was heading. I was nowhere the near the corrupts conspiracy, in the end of that melody. I was heading towards the end of that trend. Creating a burn, so I never hit the end with a warning. Centering myself, in to an entrance; purely to be taught a lesson.

On how when and where to keep everything intact. How to court claim and counteract, restoring my energy back-to-back. Giving me the upper hand to reclaim a division to the game. Restoring my energy and repeating a scheme. Just so I get back on track and redeem another theme.

For he who had a clue, had no freedom to scheme. Nor did he have the freedom nor the time out to return and redeem another theme. Because I sold them out in between. For the individual I was supposedly competing with, was the corrupts weakest Link!

Lucky me, I was given the all clear, an entrance to divide and conquer. For this time around I get in; feeding off them from within! Where every key they earned, was handed to me freely. Because the key they earned, was earned purely; for me to be saved. Because I was the one that truly earned it.

What a dream that turned out to be a drama in between. Even though, I was spoilt with ideas. I had to tread lightly bite my tongue, ever so tightly. Remain silent giving me the indication I was about to follow up on a formation. Inform me, that the destination I was handed, had already been branded.

To be continued.

AMEN

ABOUT THE AUTHOR

Panagiota Makaronis

I am not going to boast about myself, my education my family values or views. In the end what can I say life is what it is and everyone has their presentation.

What level of education I have is not important here, the fact that I have lived through death threats, dead ends, and the Demons in my head is enough for me to say! Good reddens, to hard labour.

Life to me has been nothing but expectations with several disappointments, on the hope I get somewhere trusting people when they were meant to help me was another story.

Having said that how many times have I heard people say I am helping you, I let my guard down and it ends up a never-ending Drama a story. Where if I was to repeat will end up worse than the first.

Every goal I set for myself so far though, I have achieved. This book is one of them.

But at what expense I had to endure, just so I do not lose faith in myself and in Humanity along the way. Others who knew could not wait to trace test my patience on the hope they erase my passion and end the race before me.

Because I was living and breathing in a society full of competitors, trying to compete with me and entering my realm on the hope they can harm me for they assumed that had more man power than me.

My theory is just to prove that the world is Governed, not just by everyone you meet but also by the way you witness and see yourself. It plays a huge part when you are about to end one journey and rehearse a new path.

A journey I wish not to return and replay, if anything I just want to move forward not look back and return for revenge. Because my opponent lost a fight and could not harm me so he decided to alarm everyone on the hope they cave in on it start an Allianz and harm me that way.

It left cursing the ones who were reversing and rehearsing, just so they can return stir the pot and leave me stagnant. Stuck in a world of my own sitting in self-pity, no way out unless I fought my way out.

That created more war in my peace because those who knew me, knew me well, fighting back was the only way they can prevent going through hell.

In the end all it did, was make things worse, for they were making mountains out of mole hills. However, the interpretation was enough for me to see I was on the right track the risks I took was based on not losing my faith or myself because others were doubting me and create anomaly.

They were haunted by me and my spirit they could not handle my presence or wait to see where they could hit me and run with a dead-end challenge. The only way out was to hold on to my dream repeat rebel and hit with an All might Spell.

I had come across several individuals who could not wait to break my fighting spirit, constantly on the move of how to kill me and my spirit.

The constant rejection, let down from those stalkers who had nothing better to do then follow me everywhere. Enter my realm just before I am about to make it happen, it got to the point I was failing every test because of it.

Eventually I gave in it was evident, let my Guard down on the hope and the condition there abuse and their method return and back fires.

Having to pick myself up after being pushed straight of the edge from so called Evil! Family friends and Associates, those who I call the corrupt.

What can I say a job is a job well done, level of education is based on life lessons? Everyone has a theory and so do I. Whether you agree is another story to just agree to disagree.

All the studying I did gave me an outlook, a method and outcome where sometimes I look back and wish I never entered but again I would not be here if I didn't.

The theory of here see and speak no evil to me is a lesson lived and lesson learnt. A challenge I can honestly say, it was testing a trace for me to embrace look back and erase. As I face my fears overcome another failure to that feast that handed me release.

As I look ahead and watch my journey unfold with a story untold, it will become a final phase to the next part of my truth. A challenge that will give me the indication I was on my path a feast to release peace.

Everyone is looking for answers and the hope to live

through life with comfort passion and a reason without having to deal with treason.

My memoirs are based on my journey and life lessons, it is all in the book in the end only time will tell, what can I say will be me, keeping up with the programme my way.

Not the way they state it because I hesitate to wonder who is really saving me here. For in the end the matter of facts, is in my hands, because I am an individual. My thoughts are based on my life lessons and no one can challenge or change that.

I know every challenge has its presentation and what I see is I am about to shut one door and open another. Where my vision is no longer impaired and whatever is enlisted to get to this point is no longer in the back burner.

It belongs in my spirit it is mine I earned it! I am just messenger, just passing through the rest remains Ancient History added with a Mystery.

For those who read will understand read between the lines, because my point of view is a venture to next quest on hope I can make a difference to humanity for the next generation to read and interpret my vision as a composition not a competition!

Happy Reading!

BOOKS BY THIS AUTHOR

The Theatrical Melodia Of My Life : Chronicle One

This book is based on my journey, the roller coaster I call life, my thought patterns my experiences. How I overcome so many turmoil's, how it changed my perception, for it led me towards a destination that gave me tension.

The Key To The Chronicle Of Thanatos: Chronicle 4 Krea Prea

The Key to the Chronicle of Thanatos is the continuation of my Manuscript, The Theatrical Melodia of My Life, KREA PREA!

A series of self-help books based on my journey and how I survived it. A journal built, around my thoughts and my Premonitions, where I had visions.

Crucify The Holy Spirit While You Sacrifice A Soul: Chronicle Viii

Crucify the Holy Spirit while you Sacrifice a Soul, Chronicle VIII is the continuation of the Melodia of my life KREA PREA (TM). An Epistemology, My Odyssey call it My Bible I swear by it. The difference is my one speaks in volumes and Chronicles. I speak the truth and in tongue.

The Infinite Gnostic Theism Of Evolution: Chronicle X

The infinite Gnostic Theism of Evolution Chronicle X is the continuation of my series of novella. Based on my spiritual Journey and how I perceive the world. An Autobiography and Epistemology. A memoir to advance, strengthen my wisdom and forward my knowledge, for the purpose of survival.

A Crossroads To Elevate The Spirit: Chronicle 16

A Crossroads to Elevate the Spirit, Chronicle 16; is a continuation and commemoration to the next destination. A force to be recognized, and reckoned with. Where I became, wicked, fluent; surviving on air. I was in Hiatus for way to long, I needed with passion, to find my middle ground.

www.ingramcontent.com/pod-product-compliance
Lightning Source LLC
Chambersburg PA
CBHW070734230426
43665CB00016B/2229
9781763536661